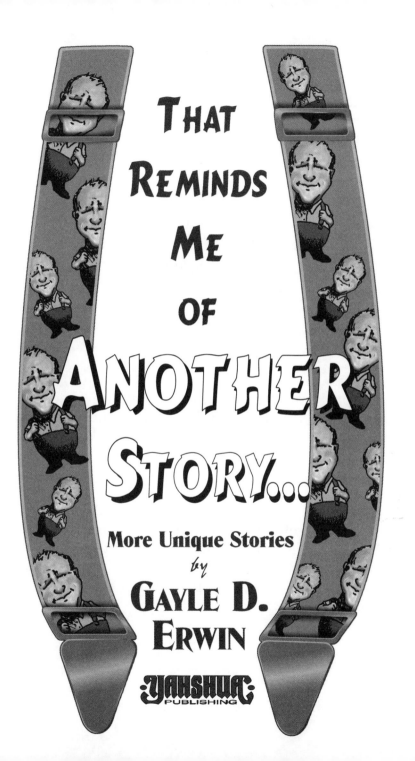

THAT REMINDS ME OF ANOTHER STORY...

More Unique Stories

by

GAYLE D. ERWIN

YAHSHUA PUBLISHING

That Reminds Me of Another Story
Copyright © 1999
ISBN 1-56599-253-9

YAHSHUA Publishing
PO Box 219
Cathedral City, CA 92235-0219
Phone 760-321-0077
FAX 760-202-1139

Scripture references, unless otherwise specified, are from the Holy Bible, King James Version (KJV).

Scripture references, where noted, are from the Holy Bible, New International Version (NIV), copyright © 1973, 1978, by the New York International Bible Society. Used by permission of Zondervan Bible Publishers.

Printed in the United States of America.

Contents

Read This First

As with my other "story book," these stories are true. Most happened to me. Some came from trusted sources. Each has a point or points. Some tell you more about me than I really want you to know. Some have an edge to them that is not the usual bent of the stories I tell; however, I have chosen to tell them because they can save you some disillusionment. Some are intended to disillusion. I believe maturity is being disillusioned and handling it properly.

All of these prove an earlier point, made in my first story book, that I live a lifetime about every ten years. Every day brings a fresh story. The only question is whether I see it or not.

I trust that as you read these to your self or to others, that you will recall your own stories that carry a point worth noting. And grow....

–Gayle D. Erwin

Markers

I am sorry to have to confess this, but there have been two people in my life whom I hated. They were both uncles. One was named Raymond and the other was named Austin.

The problem with hatred is that it binds the hater and not the hated. Hatred is a miserable set of chains that God will not leave alone in the hearts of his children. When you struggle with such emotions you often avoid beneficial interaction. I avoided the Lord's Prayer. Oh, it was mostly great except for that one line, "Forgive us our sins as we forgive those who sin against us." Ouch! Raymond and Austin kept popping into my mind.

Also, when you are in the midst of struggle, you avoid (as I did) certain passages of Scripture that you know will speak to you. You know where they are and you leave them alone conveniently limiting yourself to the Psalms where David seemed so adept at expressing strong emotions about his enemies. But, sometimes you read the Scripture accidentally. "Love your enemies!" Aargh! "Do good to those who despitefully use you." Ungh! "Pray for your enemies." Oouch!

I knew I had to do it, pray for them, but I must also admit that my early praying was not very mature. "God, you said 'vengeance was yours, you would repay.' Get them!"

But God would not let me get away with that and I knew I had to pray the kind of prayer for them that I would want prayed for me. So, I prayed, "Father, really bless them. Draw them to you and fill them with the knowledge of you and your will." You see, Austin had been the first of the Erwins to really follow the Lord, but he had drifted away and his third state was worse than his first. Raymond, also, had grown cold in his relationship with the Lord. I continued. "Bless them so much that they cannot even contain it. Overwhelm them with your goodness. Prosper them." He did!

They both returned to an intense relationship with the Lord and there was a family reconciliation that could occur only at the loving hands of God. It was wonderful. But throughout the time of praying, I noticed that I no longer hated them. In fact, to my amazement, I grew to actually love them. I knew that was God! Now, I could repeat the Lord's Prayer without hitch and without faces popping into my mind.

Well, at this point, I thought the story was over, but it wasn't.

You see, as a graduating senior from college, I made a dumb decision (neither my first nor my last). I decided that now, called by God, I with my wife and our one-year-old daughter, Gloria, would head out across America teaching in churches. Now, there isn't a great demand for kids fresh out of college to teach. What I am trying to say is that I was largely unemployed. At one time of great need, who would come to my rescue, but Raymond.

"Gayle, I need help on my farm. You can plow for me and help me care for the equipment. I will pay you, give you a place for your family to stay and you can eat at my table. I will take care of you until somebody wants you."

I thought, "What an incredible symbol of God's grace to me that it should be Raymond who would save my life. You did this didn't you, God?"

"Yep!"

"I thought so!"

Well, I thought the story was over, but it wasn't.

My father, after years of disability from his airplane accident, died in the late 1970s. Two years later, my mother married again. I performed the wedding and at the close wanted to say, "I now declare you Mom and Dad." She married one of the finest persons I have ever met—a man so like Jesus that I marvel. His name happens to be Raymond (not the same Uncle Raymond).

Again, I thought, "This is incredible, God. Now you have given me a person whom I love and respect and even call him 'Dad' and his name is Raymond. What a symbol of your reconciliation in my life. You did this, didn't you?"

"Yep!"

"I thought so."

Well, I thought the story was over, but it wasn't.

You see, there is still Austin. We had been reconciled but he moved to Northwestern Arkansas and I had not seen him for years. I didn't even know how to get in touch with him. As it happened, I spoke in a Northwest Arkansas church one Sunday. I didn't expect Austin to be there. I didn't know how to get in touch with him and I didn't know if he even knew I was around. But when I stood up to speak, there he was sitting near the back. I could not believe it. He had never before heard me teach.

When I finished, we made a beeline to each other. I can still feel the bear hug. We were brothers. All that was past was past. A few weeks after that meeting, Austin died.

Well, I thought the story was over, but it wasn't.

You see, in 1989, my oldest daughter, Gloria, gave birth to her fourth child, a son, whom she named Austin Gayle. I couldn't believe it. As I held that handsome, intelligent, outstanding... young man, I couldn't help but think, "This is incredible, God. Here in my grandson I have an ultimate symbol of your grace and reconciliation. Now our names are placed together, Austin Gayle."

"You did this, didn't you?"

"Yep!"

"I thought so!"

You see, when Gloria named him, she did not know the story I have related to you here. So, a few months after his birth, I said, "Sit down, Honey, I have a story to tell you." I told her the story you have just read. She cried and said, "Daddy, I didn't know."

"I know, Honey. That is what makes this so wonderful. This is God!"

Well, I thought the story was over, but it wasn't.

You see, six months later, I presented Austin Gayle to the Lord in dedication at the church my daughter and her family attended. As I held Austin, I stated to the congregation, "All dedications are wonderful, but there is a special story about this dedication you need to hear." I related the story to them, and, at the close, something dawned on me.

Standing three paces to my left was my step-dad, Raymond. He and my mother had flown out for this event. I realized that he had never heard his story, so I continued.

"There is another story here you need to hear." I told them Raymond's story. When I finished, we were like melted cheese all over the floor.

"Now you can see what God does when you surrender your life to Him. He finds the chains in your life, breaks them, and then fills your life with markers, symbols, altars, memorials to remind you of his great grace."

Well, I thought the story was over, but it isn't...

Questions:

1. What spiritual breakthroughs can you relate?
2. Describe a family reconciliation you have had or one you wish you had.

Coffee and Angels

At my first pastorate, an elderly, retired preacher served as one of my favorite people and staunchest supporters. His background in the denomination of his past was highly legalistic. They had preached against coffee, doctors and just about anything else. However, this brother was a few steps beyond that because of his gentle spirit and relationship with God.

He told me that he preached against drinking coffee (an official position of his denomination) until one night he dreamed of dying and going to Heaven. He described it as incredibly beautiful with angels walking around everywhere. He said that every angel he saw had a cup of coffee in his hand. After that, he never preached against coffee.

Often, when I would call a special prayer meeting, only Brother Holland would show up, so he and I would pray together. One prayer that flowed from his gentle spirit scared me. I lacked the freedom to pray that prayer. He would pray, "God, if I am going to damage any of your children or hurt any of your little lambs, just kill me now and take me home." I envied his prayer but lacked the bravery.

Questions:

1. How would you describe your bravest prayer?
2. What "rules" have changed in your life because of new insight?

Coffee and Orphans

Six weeks after the overthrow of the vicious Ceaucescu government in Romania, I joined a team of people taking a truck load of supplies into that country. It was my most direct people-to-people experience in an outright Communist country. Although they were now free, they did not know how to act in freedom. In each town that we stayed, we were quizzed and treated like suspicious people simply because that was the way they were trained to treat all outsiders.

Ceaucescu was so paranoid that he destroyed all means of communication among the people. It was illegal to have a copying machine or a typewriter. Having a telephone made you a source of suspicion as would travel. His dreaded secret police kept everyone in terror.

We could travel only as far into the country as our supply of gasoline would permit since no lead-free gasoline existed there. Brasov was our turn around point for delivering supplies and we headed out with our last stop planned in the city of Arad.

Unable to find the intended person for our final drop of supplies, our leader said there was an orphanage in the same town we could visit. This was a state-run orphanage that happened to have a Christian as the director. She was a very educated person who held a high position in the country until she refused to denounce her faith, so

Ceaucescu relegated her to what amounted to a work Siberia—directing an orphanage. Sadly, these orphanages, like their hospitals had almost no supplies. The rooms were stark and toys were absent.

Ceaucescu demanded that his people have children and that demand resulted in large, unsupportable families with many abandoned babies. Ceaucescu himself would use the blood of babies to give himself "youth producing" transfusions.

Our visit to the orphanage was highly welcomed by the director and the staff as we toured the building. My heart was torn by sympathy for the children and disgust at Ceaucescu. At the close of our tour, the director brought us back to her office and treated us to a cup of coffee. We all looked at each other and exclaimed, "Coffee!?" We knew that coffee was like gold in that country. It virtually did not exist.

We inquired. With a little embarrassment, she told us that she had been saving the coffee to give a cup to each staff member as a Christmas present (this was February), but they were so delighted to have us there that they wanted to give us their best.

You can imagine how we felt as we held their best in our hands and sipped. Then we looked at each other and our faces lit up. We remembered that supplies still remained in our truck and that under the front seat was six pounds of coffee. Hey, we had a party giving that to the director of the orphanage. I couldn't help but remember the words of Jesus, "Give and it will be given unto you...."

Questions:

1. Have you ever been given great hospitality when you knew it was very costly to the giver? Describe.
2. Has anyone ever thought you were an angel because you did something amazing for them? Tell about it.

Turning Points

Why Is He Mad at Me?

A child too young to read delivered one of my greatest lessons. Forgive me, but I choose not to describe my early style of speaking, but I will tell you of a change that occurred. A local family in South Louisiana visited our church one Sunday. Because of their background, it was a remarkable event. The family included several small children.

Some days later from a mutual friend, I heard something that shook me and changed me deeply. On the way home, the four-year-old daughter of the visiting family asked her mother a question. "Why was that man mad at me?"

"He wasn't mad at you."

"Yes, he was. Why was he mad at me?"

"He wasn't mad at you. Why do you think that?"

"Well, if he wasn't mad at me, then why did he yell at me like that?"

My heart was grieved when I heard that. It changed me. I never want a child to leave my presence and think that in the Name of Jesus I was mad at them.

I Don't Understand a Thing

I was attending a local university to complete my master's degree, and, at the same time, serving as pastor of a church. At the close of the service, I habitually stood at the back and greeted people as they left. One precious, elder saint who had been part of the church for 60 years and whom I loved and appreciated, approached me to say goodbye.

"Pastor, we love you so much."

"Thank you."

"You are so eloquent. We love to hear you preach."

"Thank you." I was loving this.

"But, Pastor...."

"Yes?"

"I don't understand a word you say."

I gulped as she continued.

"We know you are intelligent and that you go to the university and we are proud of that, but you use these long university words and I don't understand a word you say."

I thanked her for telling me and then went home and licked my wounds as I realized that I had fallen into the trap of arrogance and ego. I pledged to make myself understandable to anyone. Children as well as little old ladies (and men).

Questions:

1. Name two people who have influenced your life and tell how they did.
2. What have been some specific turning points in your life?

That's My God

Ezekiel Guti thanked me profusely for taking him to Universal Studios theme park in California. Guti, founder of a very large organization of black churches in Zimbabwe, was not excited about the rides or other shows. He especially appreciated the knowledge of how they fooled our eyes and made things seem to be something that they were not.

He explained, "My people are not sophisticated enough to know that this is trickery. They think that what they see on the movie screen is what actually happened. This is wonderful that I can go back and tell them the truth."

I tell you this to introduce another event of great proportions. Another friend, Bruce Coble, went from Tennessee to Zimbabwe to serve as the director of Guti's Bible College. He became a much-loved person to the students. On one of his trips back to the United States, Bruce collected some of his favorite videotapes to take back and show to the students. The tapes included Hollywood's version of *The Ten Commandments*. The classic scene in the movie is the parting of the Red Sea. Bruce found it difficult to tell me this story without choking up with tears, but he said that when the students saw that depiction on the screen, as far as they knew, the camera was actually there recording the scene. They got so excited that they were all standing on their chairs shouting, "That's my God! That's my God!"

Such straightforward love of God!

Questions:

1. How do you feel about media attempts to portray Bible miracles?
2. When do you get the most excited about God?

Birth

The birth of a baby is such an awesome thing. Every couple must wonder at each birth, "Will everything be OK? Will the baby be healthy? Can our combined bodies produce something good?" Anxious moments accompany every birth.

Our first three children, all daughters, provided much joy for us and I would have been a totally happy man, but my wife and I decided to have our final child when we reached age 30. I confess that, as a man, I desired to have a son; however, I would have still been deliriously happy with another daughter.

The time came for the delivery. My wife delivers children rather rapidly and I was glad that we lived just five minutes from the hospital.

I waited those anxious moments. Modern times with the husband assisting the wife in the delivery room had not yet arrived. Hospitals still considered husbands just next to leprosy, so I waited a safe distance away, but close enough to observe the action of the birthing department.

At the moment that I expected our child to be born, I noticed a flurry of activity that obviously came from near panic. My anxiety increased and I began to pray in new ways. Now, I was building a new plane of acceptance with the Lord in terms of our child. If there were dangers to life or health, I would accept and grow with that; however, I prayed that it would not be so. If there were dangers to my wife, I would accept that; but again, I prayed that it was not so.

Long moments left me in my state of anxiety and prayer. Then finally the news came that our healthy son had been born. Only then, on inquiry, did I find that the tragedy belonged to someone else as their baby had died. I accepted our new joy with mixed feelings.

I also discovered that some of that activity came from the nurses moving about looking for materials to make flags in the delivery room, since our son, Clyde, was born on Flag Day. Nonetheless, I pondered for some while my resolution with God during that anxious time.

Questions:

1. Describe the tensions and anxieties you experience in having a child (or sibling).
2. How do you accept your own genetic difficulties?

Black Market

There once existed two very powerful radio stations just over the Texas border in Mexico. Whatever else they broadcast, late at night, various indescribable religious programming ruled and reached most of the Central USA. Often, when I had finished my nighttime studies in college and was winding down for bed, I would turn on one of those stations just for the grins.

One particular speaker regaled us with his prowess. I write it here as I heard it. "I have the gift of prophecy. I know *everthang.* Just write me and ask me. I know the secret of the *hygerdren* bomb."

I thought, "Well, you know everything except the English you speak."

Another broadcaster's story requires a little background. One of the "tent evangelists" of the 1950s purchased a place in Arizona and named it "Miracle Valley." Those were the days of "can you top this?" So, another evangelist, a woman, decided to buy a place that she named "Miracle Mountain." I enjoyed listening to her because I knew what was going on and it gave a few extra chuckles. She, too, claimed prophetic inspiration and would make LP recordings of her prophecies which you could have by enclosing an offering to keep her on the air.

Now, I need to give a little more background. Some who read this have no idea what an LP is. That is what we called a "long playing" record.

Perhaps in this CD world, you don't even know what a "record" is. Well, the audiotechnical world progressed from flat 12-inch disks with grooves on them in which a needle would rest as the disk revolved at 78 revolutions per minute. The next stage was a 7-inch disk that revolved at 45 revolutions per minute. Finally, audio perfection seemed to have come in the 33⅓ RPM "long play" that carried much higher fidelity. Forgive me for what seems an unnecessary explanation, but there is a reason.

Long play connoisseurs knew that, for some strange reason, in the "pressing" of the records, one could hear at the very beginning a phantom image of the sound just before the actual recording began. Now, knowing that, let's return to the lady evangelist.

One of the records of the prophecies she offered over the air apparently had that "ghost image" flaw in it when the pressing was completed. Here is how she handled it.

"If you will send me an offering, I will send you this special recording of prophecies just for you. At the beginning, if you will listen closely, you will hear the voice of Jesus as he begins to tell me what to say."

Enough. Bedtime.

Questions:

1. Have you ever watched or listened to any religious programming simply because you couldn't believe it? For instance?
2. Describe any religious competitiveness you have observed.

Weddings

The bride plans to the finest detail to insure that her wedding proceeds flawlessly. However, flawless weddings are immensely forgettable. The little hitches, the laughable moments are the items talked about into the future and are the triggers that bring recall of the event. But no, and I emphasize NO bride ever plans the glitches. Yet, I can assure you that glitches always happen. They may not always be obvious to the audience and they may not have happened publicly, but they always happen. Two events stand out in my own memory of weddings with glitches that could never have been planned. One happened to a friend and I let you hear it first.

The Lisp

After years of difficult and slow productivity of ministry in a pastorate, God had given a harvest of local people to this pastor friend of mine. About six months after this revival, the pastor was performing a wedding in the parsonage between a young lady who had grown up in his church and a man who was a newcomer product of the revival. Before I go on, I must tell you that my pastor friend, a giant of a man physically and spiritually, speaks with a slight lisp that varies in intensity.

Friends and family surrounded the couple as the pastor proceeded with the ceremony. At one point, he instructed the man to "clasp hands." Unfortunately, the pastor's lisp changed "clasp" enough that the misunderstanding groom, unaccustomed to these new ways, began to clap his hands. The pastor, a bit flustered by it all, knew that the bride would understand, so he attempted to correct it by telling her to "clasp hands."

She misunderstood, also, and began to clap her hands. By now, the pastor realized that if you can't whip them, join them, so he laid his Bible down and began to clap his hands and loudly praise the Lord. The crowd joined in and after this brief happy moment, when the pastor quit clapping, everybody quit. He then took up his Bible and continued the ceremony to the end.

No Counseling

I didn't recognize the voice on the phone asking me if I performed weddings. I responded positively but told the female caller that I required at least three hours of counseling prior to the ceremony. After what seemed to be a long pause, she responded that they would do that, so I began to question further. My first question was, "How old are you?"

She responded, "Sixty-five."

"Forget the counseling," I replied. (I was only 25 anyway. What could I tell her?)

When she identified herself, I realized that she was the vegetable farmer who lived a distance away and managed to come to church only about once a month. I remembered she was a widow.

The ceremony was scheduled to occur at her sister's house in the town where I lived.

The day arrived. I knocked on the door of her sister's house and she excitedly answered and invited me in. She then hollered out of each side of the house to neighbors who came over to be the legal witnesses as required in that state. She then yelled out of the back door into a large plowed field. A lone figure was working about 200 yards away.

The worker, about 70 years old, walked in, brushed the dust off his overalls and the groom was now ready for the wedding. The ceremony was uneventful except that the bride misunderstood when I said to take his right hand. She thought I said to shake his right hand, so she pumped it vigorously.

When the ceremony was over, I discovered that the bride and I were the only literate people present. I had to sign for the witnesses and for the groom.

I chuckled at the situation, not knowing that this day would bring about an additional story. (see "What Will Two Dollars Get?")

Questions:

1. If you are married, what "went wrong" during your ceremony that you still vividly remember? Do you remember that event better than the ceremony itself?
2. How would you design the perfect wedding?

Benevolent Robbery

I Can Cook

On my first trip to Rhodesia (now Zimbabwe) my relationship with the national black people suffered a strain or two. As I walked along, they insisted on carrying my briefcase or my Bible for me. Being a capable American and a person who opposed seeing them as slaves or underlings, I resisted this service as firmly as I could. Often I succeeded. Often I failed. In my insensitivity, I failed to notice their fallen faces when I succeeded. I remember thinking that I was teaching them a thing or two about Americans and how I viewed them as I resisted. They silently accepted.

The following year, I returned, accompanied by a pastor friend, to teach at a leadership conference. They pitched a large meeting tent in a church campground and lodged my friend and me in a very nice cabin. One of the ladies cooked breakfast for us in the kitchen of the cabin. After only one day of this, we, as capable American guys, informed her that she need not return the next day—we could make our own breakfast and let her sleep later in the morning. On the next morning, we cooked and the lady did not return.

At lunch the next day, I detected a distance, an aloofness that had changed from the day before. I mentioned to the wife of the leader, "I guess you know that we made our own breakfast this morning." She nodded somewhat icily. Immediately, I knew this must be pursued.

"Is that a problem?"

"Yes."

"What kind of problem is it?"

"If you don't let us cook your breakfast for you, you are robbing us of a blessing."

"Please tell her we want her to come back tomorrow."

"Okay."

Now that the air was cleared, everyone brightened and conversation flowed. Now, when people approached me to carry my briefcase or Bible I quickly smiled and relented.

Don't Be Stingy

One other area of my cultural thinking waited to slap me around. At the time I first visited Zimbabwe, the white people could hire a full time black worker to handle the yard and other exterior household duties for $35 a month and could hire another person, usually a lady, to cook and care for the interior of the house for another $35. For that paltry sum, a person of any means at all could live a luxurious and easy life.

I bristled and considered this life style to be taking advantage of the local people. I mentioned to the black leader that if I lived here I would not hire someone at that wage. I would take care of my household myself. He did not answer. By now, I had learned that such silence spoke volumes and decided I should chase this thought.

"How would you feel about a white person living here and doing his own work?"

"We would think he was stingy."

"Why is that?"

"We understand that you have a lot more money than we do and it does not bother us, but we need the work. If you don't hire us, then we are unemployed. We know you can afford to hire us, so if you don't, we think you are stingy."

Another of my pet arrogances crashed.

Questions:

1. To what degree can you let people do things for you that you are capable of doing yourself?

2. What customs of foreign countries or foreigners in your country have you found surprising or intriguing?

What Are You Trying to Teach Me?

I scooted along on the icy Missouri freeway in our new van just purchased from a cousin's dealership. Our kids chose to ride home with me while my wife, Ada, drove the old car, which we intended to sell on the open market.

As we drove along, I constantly monitored Ada in the rear view mirror making sure she was OK and following along. As I reached the bottom of a long slope, I glanced in the mirror and could not see her. I slowed down to see if she would catch up. She didn't. I pulled off and looked back. I entered the world of shock. On top of the hill behind us her overturned car lay on its roof in the middle of the highway with smoke and steam billowing out.

I instructed the kids to stay in the van while I raced the half mile back up to the car. Each step was a death step to me. My heart pounded. Along the way, questions raced through my mind: "What did I do wrong that this is happening to me? Where have I not been faithful? Did I fail to pay my tithes somewhere? Have my thoughts been out of control? What are you trying to teach me?"

All these questions remained unresolved as I raced along. They simply hung there haunting me. As I neared the top of the hill, I looked up and saw Ada standing out beside the road. I raced to embrace her and check, "Are you OK?"

She was totally unhurt except for glass slivers in her hands.

So, I did learn something. I learned that my questions were totally irrelevant.

Questions:

1. When has something happened to you that caused you to ask "Why?"
2. What do you think God requires of you in order to bless you? What does "the grace of God" mean to you?

Office Walls

The walls around my cubicle came about neck high. Status, not efficiency, dictated that. I worked on the headquarters staff of a denomination developing magazines for the youth department.

I quickly learned after I arrived that one's status could be determined by the height of his wall. Secretaries had no wall at all. The next level up, the lowest executives, had walls neck high. The director of a department such as the youth department had walls that came within a foot or so of the ceiling; however, they were walls of the same material as mine.

The executive over several departments had walls all the way to the ceiling; however, they were made of the same material as mine. Finally, when you reached the highest level of executive, one not only had walls to the ceiling made of normal frame wall material, but he also had carpet. Now the status was dependent upon where the office was located in relationship to the number one guy and the actual size of the office.

When a school was built onto the headquarters building, it was discovered at the completion of the building that the headmaster of the new school would have an office with ten square feet more than the top executive. Many thousands of dollars were spent to reduce the size of that office so protocol would not be violated.

But back to my own walls. A friend of mine said that they wanted to give me walls appropriate to my status, but they felt I would keep tripping over them.

Questions:

1. Describe some "status symbols" that you observe on your job.
2. What symbols of position or achievement do you have?

CATastrophe

The scene: An upscale Los Angeles suburban house.
The characters: A retired couple.

They awakened to the sound of a kitten crying. The crying continued throughout their early morning coffee disturbing them enough to check it out. He discovered that a kitten had climbed to the tip of a tree in their yard and could not get down. They knew they couldn't leave it crying there, so emergency procedures took over.

Not being milk drinkers, they rushed to buy a quart and placed a saucer full at the base of the tree to lure the kitten. The crying continued. The cat stayed. Next he placed a ladder against the tree and climbed to the top of the ladder. Unfortunately, the tree was a fairly young one and could not support his weight at the top to reach the kitten.

Discouraged they sat down and pondered what to do next as the crying continued. "Ah, I know," he exclaimed. "Remember when we were kids and in school we read about the fire department coming and rescuing cats from trees? Let's call the fire department!"

An unsympathetic voice answered, "Look, this is Los Angeles. We don't get cats down from trees. That occurs only in rural places. You will have to get the cat down by yourself."

Discouraged further, they returned to another cup of coffee in the miserable sound of this kitten crying. Then, enlightenment! "I know what to do, Honey," the man said. "I will climb the ladder as high as I can against the tree and tie a rope. Then I will attach the other end of the rope to the bumper of the car. Since this is a young and supple tree, it should bend easily as I back up the car. You can get on the hood and when the tree is low enough, retrieve the cat."

It worked! The tree bent nicely and just as the lady reached up to get the cat, the rope broke! Meeeeoooooooowww....... That cat was launched. I guess this is where the word "catapult" comes from...or perhaps "catastrophe." They had no idea where the cat was "pulted." Now they sat feeling worse than before about what they had done to the poor kitty.

Several days later, while at the grocery store, they encountered a recently widowed neighbor from several houses away. They noticed that she was buying cat food. "We didn't know you had a cat."

"Well, I didn't until just a few days ago. You know, I have been so lonely since my husband died and I was out in the back yard praying, 'God, should I buy a dog or a cat to help keep me company?' when out of the sky this cat fell right into my yard!"

Questions:

1. Have you ever seen God accomplish something and it appeared that He might have
   been also having fun?
2. Have you ever had something seem to go
   wrong but turn out so right?

Seeds of Revolution

If the Truth Were Known

My second visit to Africa delivered almost more revelation and disillusionment than I was prepared to handle. At the time, Rhodesia (later changed to Zimbabwe) suffered deeply from a long civil war. The 250,000 white people were fighting hard to stay in power and keep the 8 million blacks from ruling the country. The fly in the ointment was the backing of the black cause by Communist China. The white government with freer access to the western press fully exploited this Communist backing in seeking favor and support from the rest of the world.

The honesty and openness of a handful of knowing people in the country handed me a mountain of awesome and devastating knowledge. One black leader informed me that Africa could never be Communist. "Africans believe in God. Communism doesn't," he informed me. "They can never take our belief away. Also, we Africans invented communal living, so the Communists have nothing to teach us in that area."

Then he dropped the bombshell on me. "We love the United States and sought your help to gain freedom in our revolution just as you had in yours, but you turned us down. The Chinese and Russians were only too glad to help us and we had to have help. Our cost for this is that you consider us to be Communists like them."

I then began to see the power of publicity connections. The white government gave glowing accounts in press releases of their "Christian" leaning while warning us that if the blacks won, the Bible would no longer be taught in schools. What they did not tell us was that there were no schools for blacks except those schools provided by missionaries. Government information suppliers further advertised that on Friday nights they had a required prayer meeting for their military troops. We Americans, of course, were impressed with that.

From the lips of a white person, I learned the truth about that prayer meeting on Friday nights. It was not a prayer meeting at all, but instead a strip show to entertain the troops, but that obviously could not be related to the press.

But let's return to the school situation. After the war and the black government was in power, I observed two things, one of them devastating and the other thrilling. First, the devastating. After speaking one Sunday at a church in a "Township," which is a large black settlement but generally not on maps, and as we drove back to where I was staying, we passed a building surrounded by a high barbed-wire fence. The building was brick and windowless. Outside the fence, women gathered as if waiting to go inside. A policeman or two wandered among the women.

Immediately, I recognized what this had to be—a prison. I simply remarked to my friends in the car that I guess you had to have prisons in Zimbabwe, also. Hesitantly and with embarrassment, they corrected me. "No, Brother Gayle. This is a beer hall. They are all over the country. In the past the government supplied us with very cheap beer to keep us drunk and happy. When drunkenness is involved, violence breaks out and they just lock us in like a prison to let us fight it out. These women are here trying to get their husbands out and save their homes. Now, under the new government, we are converting these halls to schools since we don't have any school buildings, but this one is still a beer hall."

Now, the thrilling. A year later, I took two friends from California with me to see what was happening in the country. One was a school teacher anxious to see what the schools would be like under this new "Communist" government. I told them not to make too many pre-judgments. I encouraged them to simply drop in on a school and spend a few hours.

They were welcomed. When they returned, they could not contain themselves. "Every class hour began with Bible reading and prayer and sometimes a devotional for the whole school over the intercom," they informed me.

I smiled and joked, "I guess they are not as advanced as we are in the United States."

Fruit of Apartheid

The scene in South Africa was equally as difficult. I shall never forget a time when a leading black Christian sought my counsel. "A major Christian organization has asked me to come to work for them. I would really love to do it, but I don't know if I can afford it."

"Why is that? Is the pay a lot lower than what you are making on your job now?"

"Oh, no! The pay is much better, but I would lose nine years."

"Lose nine years? What do you mean?"

"Well, here in South Africa, blacks are not permitted to purchase a home until they have been working for the same employer for ten years. I have been with this employer for nine years and if I change jobs, I have to start all over."

"But if you can't purchase a home, what do you do? Where do you live?"

"The employers provide dormitories for the men, but the wives have to stay back in the homelands. The men have to be away from their wives most of the time. It is very difficult and causes a lot of problems."

My heart broke. Over and over the words of Jesus rang in my ears, "The Spirit of the Lord is upon me...to set at liberty those who are oppressed."

Questions:

1. What things do you know that you would like to shout from the housetops?
2. When do you feel the press has lied to you or misrepresented news?

May I Pretend?

As an assistant pastor overwhelmed by the counseling load, I gathered my most frequent visitors into a small home fellowship to increase the spiritual dynamics that bring healing. Among those in attendance was a young lady convinced by the constant assurance of prior church experience that she was demon possessed, who struggled with her sexual identity and who wrapped all of this in a body afflicted with cerebral palsy. She, others and I joined, making our home fellowship very interesting.

Occasionally, Martha (not her real name) would wander off into a sinful situation, then defiantly call me on the phone and tell me where she was, then ask, "What do you think of me now?" I would always assure her that though she knew how I felt about what she was doing, I still loved her and this broke my heart. She would go silent and then hang up the phone.

In spite of these moments, so many wonderful things happened in her life that her husband asked if he could join our home fellowship. He felt that the group could help him with some abiding problems in his life. We welcomed him.

Martha still had far to go. Her fuse burned hot and quick. When it reached the powder of her agitation, she would blow up and read the riot act to me and describe me in ways my mother would not appreciate. Her temper was simply one of the many things she struggled with while never losing her faith in God. She added to the adventure of my life as I rejoiced in the degree of her growth.

After I left her city to take another assignment in the kingdom, I had no further contact with her until the pastor of the church called me fairly early one morning. Martha had entered a major hospital for heart surgery and the pastor traveled to be with her. When he arrived and greeted her, she asked him if he minded if she pretended that he was Gayle Erwin. He smiled and said, "Go ahead."

Immediately she exploded and added him to the list of those whose mothers would not appreciate the commentary. When she finished, she thanked him and said, "I needed that." When they wheeled her into the operating room, he immediately called me and related the story.

Sometimes being chewed out can be a good thing.

Questions:

1. What difficult relationships have you had that worked out to be very profitable?
2. How do you feel when someone loses their temper and calls you bad things?

College

I always wanted to be a medical doctor from the early years of my life, but the whole prospect of going to college seemed decidedly remote. My parents invented poverty. Life in the survival mode overruled the discretionary mode that afforded college.

Further discouragement came from the fact that I was not in the upper 10% of my class in terms of grades. Academic scholarships seemed out of the question. However, two events changed all that.

A new scholarship program called "National Merit Scholarships" issued its first 200 national scholarships in my senior year. Unfortunately, candidates were limited to the top 10% of each senior class. Consequently, I sought programs that did not have such limits. Another major scholarship program was the "General Motors National Scholarship Program." This program accepted any candidate, but only 100 of those were issued each year in the nation.

I consulted with a Tulane University representative and he told me to forget the General Motors scholarship because they were all political and I could never win one. Undaunted but a bit shaken by his discouragement, I forged ahead and began the process of application and testing for the GM scholarship during my senior year.

Shortly after beginning the General Motors process, my school principal informed me that I was chosen to take the first National Merit test. I quizzed him on how this unbelievable opportunity occurred. He winked and said, "We have ways."

Now, the reason this was even important to me was the fact that these were the kinds of scholarships that paid the difference between what I could pay for college and the total cost of whatever school I chose to attend. For me, that meant a full-ride scholarship.

To my amazement, after the tests were taken for both programs, I received a letter informing me that I qualified for the second round of testing for each. (This was before the magazine prize people, so it was believable.) For one of the scholarships, it meant another SAT-type test. For the other, a thorough description of my life and goals in an essay. When the testing was completed, no recourse remained except to wait. I waited.

My principal called me into his office one day along with four other students—all of them mental giants. In front of him was a letter sent to him by the National Merit people listing all of us as finalists. His mysterious way bothered me as he discussed the letter. He informed us that he was not permitted to actually tell us what was in the letter but he was going to see if, somehow, he could influence the final results and get scholarships for more of us. I knew that if any one could do it, he could. He did inform us that the letter listed one person as a scholar and the other four as finalists, but he would tell us nothing more.

This was a bit tough on me since I was desperate and the other finalists were financially capable of going to college.

No such information arrived concerning the General Motors scholarship since it used a different system and I was the only one in the school competing. My thoughts could not dwell on all of it because of studies and the fact that a new love had come into my life and was taking up mental time. Also, I had been invited to enter the Elks Club State Youth Leadership award contest and that had an immediate $150 prize if won. That amount represented a fortune at that time to me.

As Spring advanced toward its middle, my parents decided to take a trip to Georgia to attend a church gathering and left us two older sons to fend for ourselves in their absence, but not before making up a mountain of frozen hamburger patties. That was all my brother and I needed to survive and survive well. Two days after they left and I was home alone, the phone rang and the man asked to speak to Gayle Erwin. He identified himself and informed me that I had been chosen as a National Merit Scholar in its premier year and they wanted to know if I had settled on a college. I told him that I chose to go to Millsaps College in Jackson, Mississippi. I was euphoric.

College financial concerns disappeared. Just minutes after I hung up the phone, it rang again and the person calling informed me that I had received the Elks Club award and wanted to set up a time to present it and the check in a public ceremony. Euphoria squared.

Minutes later, the phone rang again. This time, a General Motors Scholarship representative called to inform me that I had won one of their national scholarships. Now, it was euphoria to the tenth power. No one was at home to share this news. My adrenaline flowed so fast, I took off and walked all over town just to handle the energy. I also needed to give it some time and come back to determine if I simply had a dream or if this could possibly be true.

Part of my unusual dilemma was the scholarships. I could not take them both. They were each exclusive because they provided all college expenses. Which one should I choose. It would be heady to be part of the very first National Merit winners (many were featured in Life Magazine), yet the General Motors scholarship gave a larger bonus to the college for having me as a student and would permit me to change colleges if I so desired.

I decided that the honor was not worth the other options and chose the General Motors scholarship. For a number of reasons, I was glad I did.

One was the fact that GM sent an executive to meet with me every year and see how I was doing as well as take me to a fine restaurant to eat (that was very educational). Another reason was that they were not concerned that I got married in my sophomore year. A third reason came at the end of my college years. Out of gratitude, I decided that I would purchase one of the new Chevrolet Corvair rear-engine cars since I desperately needed a car.

When I informed the executive, he quickly said, "Don't do it." He said it was a bad car and for me to leave it alone. Some time later, Ralph Nader independently confirmed the warning. More gratitude!

Questions:

1. How would you describe the difficulties you went through to achieve your education?
2. When can you remember being euphoric in your life?

Coming by the Truckloads

In the mid 1960s I participated in a program called Clinical Pastoral Education conducted by the chaplain at a mental hospital. The study offered a number of insights that I now value. A startling event I observed merits this story.

Having completed counseling in a medium security ward, I made my way toward the outside door. Beds were being wheeled into the hallway. I asked a psychiatrist standing nearby if they were emptying the rooms for remodeling. His reply shocked me.

"No, we are preparing for a large influx of patients tonight."

"Really? Why?" I queried. "Is it a phase of the moon or something?"

"Oh, no," he chuckled. "This is the last night of a holy-roller camp meeting on the north edge of town. Whatever happens there, for some reason they will be bringing people in here by the truckloads."

My initial embarrassment at his words (I knew how they felt about expressive religion in general) quickly faded and was replaced by understanding. I knew immediately what the problem was and why so many would crack up and have to be institutionalized.

This camp meeting was run every summer by a church denomination that is referred to by many as a "Oneness" group. That means they believe there is no Trinity and all expressions of God, be it Father, Son or Holy Spirit, are merely Jesus by some other manifestation. Along with that, they are strongly pentecostal in experience.

Two specific theologies set the stage for the last-night crisis that would overflow a mental institution. They believe that in order to be saved, you must be baptized in Jesus' Name only and also speak in tongues. They base this belief on an extreme interpretation of Acts 2:38. Here is how it destroyed people.

A significant number of people who had salvation experiences with God and were even "appropriately" baptized, felt that they remained unsaved because they had not managed to speak in tongues. All sorts of good things had happened to them in their seeking for God and they loved God and wanted to serve Him, but they simply had not spoken in tongues, the final proof and seal of their salvation.

So, now, in spite of their earnest seeking, the camp had come to the end and they were not "saved." It was more than they could handle; not knowing what else to do and because of the extremity of their theology, the Heavens seemed locked to them. They cracked and were hauled off for treatment.

What an unforeseen tragedy for such an extreme theology.

Questions:

1. Have you been or have you seen anyone dam-
   aged by extreme religious demands? What
   was the result?
2. What do you understand God's requirements
   for salvation to be?

We Tried the Gayle Erwin Method

I broke my pledge to myself never to speak at such an event again and accepted the invitation to a youth rally for a certain denomination. So much destructive tradition controlled the meeting that one could barely call it a rally, much less for youth.

I arrived and sat by invitation on the platform with a group of about ten pastors. We were all dressed to the hilt in suits and ties. The young people sat in small galaxies of their own clumped around the edges of the auditorium. Each pastor was introduced and lauded while the competitive forms carefully calculated by each youth leader were being tallied to see which group would go as the "winner." I grew sicker by the moment.

Finally, the awards were presented with much fanfare but received with total disinterest. The time had come for me to speak. I was renewing my promise to myself never to do this again.

I walked to the pulpit and apologized to the young people for what I felt was going on. I told them that first of all, I felt very removed from them and it was unfair for them to relocate, so I would. I made my way past various obstacles down to the front and continued. "Further," I told them, "I am most uncomfortable in this suit and tie, especially since they only exist on the platform, so if you don't mind I will take off my coat and tie." I ripped them off and threw them aside.

The place was electrified. Attention grew beyond each galaxy and I had their focus for the next 45 minutes. Everyone took note of what had happened. I left to go home and promptly forgot the whole event.

Months later, a friend told me an unbelievable story. Going the rounds was the statement, "We tried the Gayle Erwin Method and it didn't work." You see, at the next rally, all of the pastors, having observed what I did and what happened, conspired to, at a certain moment, all get up, say they were coming down front and rip off their coats and ties. They were put off by the laughter. So, the "Gayle Erwin Method" didn't work. I am so glad.

Questions:

1. When have you ever used the phrase "They got it all wrong," or "They just don't get it"?
2. How do you feel when you are misunderstood?

Wineskins

The skin of an arctic white fox adorns our house as a decoration. On a trip to the northern edge of Alaska, the Christian Eskimo who trapped it sold it to me. (Only Eskimos were allowed to trap these animals.) I asked him how to care for it. Should I have it tanned? What preservatives will I need? His answer surprised me.

He said that the best thing would be to play with it a lot with your hands. The oils from your hands and the flexing alone would keep the skin soft and pliable. We did what he said and the results were as he predicted.

I thought of that in terms of the wineskins of the Church. Perhaps we get set in our ways so quickly that stiffness sets in. How do you change that? Play with it. Flex it a lot. Massage its schedules. Keep your hands on it.

Questions:

1. Have you participated in the founding of a church? What were some of the difficult things that you now miss?
2. How would you like to "play with" the church schedule or building program?

Cuban Missile Crisis

Do you remember the Cuban Missile Crisis? Or are you just too stinkin' young? As Kruschev and Kennedy stared each other down, our country panicked. We knew we were going to nuclear war.

At the time, I was a pastor at the mouth of the Mississippi River, 85 miles below New Orleans, and many people don't know that there is an 85 miles below New Orleans, but there is. This alluvial peninsula jutts out toward Cuba and we knew we were in jeopardy.

My phone began to ring. "Pastor, it looks like it is all over. I need to get saved. Tell me how."

"OK." Talk...talk...talk....

Ring—Saved

Ring—Saved

Ring—Saved....

Unfortunately, the crisis was over before Sunday.

I realized that I (we) do my most intense praying when I am in crisis. It's too dry...let's pray. It's too wet...let's pray. We are near war...let's pray. The economy is bad...let's pray. Sometimes I will hear, "Things are so bad there is nothing left to do but pray." Never do I hear, "I just inherited $10 million...we need to pray."

Luke 5:16 notes that Jesus, at the height of his success, often withdrew into the wilderness to pray. He understood. We are never more vulnerable than when we are prosperous. We are never in greater need of prayer. That is why God had to warn the Children of Israel as they entered the promised land that when they had harvested crops they didn't sow and eaten from trees they didn't plant to beware lest they forget the Lord.

Questions:

1. What promises have you made to God during a crisis?
2. What crisis in your life drove you to the most intense prayer?

Distant Disdain

She hated me. We had never met and she did not know me nor would she have recognized me in a crowd, but she hated me. I discovered this in a Chicago area church 1,700 miles away from where I lived. As she confessed this to me, my heart joined her as she related her tortuous journey to this incredible moment.

Now, a great distance from where her disdain began, she developed her own relationship with the Lord and in counseling with her pastor came to realize that her feelings toward me needed to be resolved in confession and forgiveness. I spoke at her new home church, and she gathered the courage to speak to me personally.

Years before while staying in a home on the west coast and during some of the more rebellious times of her life, the man of the house gave her a copy of *The Jesus Style* and told her that this might help her. She took the gift as an insult, grudgingly read the book, growing to hate the author and the giver with each page. That grudge drove her out of the home and far away as her rebellion bore its fruit.

Finally, the sum of the messages that resounded in her heart won and she realized that she truly needed God in her life. That event led to the event on this evening in church. She gingerly told me the story and asked me to forgive her and wanted me to know that she didn't hate me any more. I told her that this was a "first" for me and that she was definitely forgiven. I mused that there might be many more who, when reading *The Jesus Style* might find its message such a confrontation to their lifestyle and thought that perhaps a whole army out there hates me.

Ah, well. They are already forgiven. Just so they read.

Questions:

1. Have you ever been surprised to discover someone's reaction to you?
2. What reaction have you had to someone that has kept you from really knowing them?

Eddies

I remember well the sickening feeling I would sometimes get in the pit of my stomach on the relaxing rides my family and I would take along the Mississippi River levee in Venice, Louisiana. On occasion we would spot a crowd standing or sitting anxiously along the river bank as they watched small boats slowly weave a thorough pattern in the water dragging fishhooks behind them.

The river had claimed another victim and they were dragging for the body.

The mainstream of the river was dangerous, but everyone knew that, so appropriate precautions were taken when sailing its waters. Conversely, the dangers of the whirlpools and eddies along the bank seemed minute and were often ignored to the tragic peril of the swimmer or wader.

I pondered that and thought of a spiritual application. Revival represents the mainstream of the river. Along the edge of every river and every revival arise smaller whirlpools and eddies of sometimes-heretical activity or sometimes-cultic activity that may seem benign or often ignored to the peril of those whose feet enter. Perhaps, because of the apparently faster moving water of the whirlpool, a strange attraction grows that this might be a good adventure. Later, a caring community grieves during the dragging process.

Occasionally, someone would be rescued alive, but the absence of lifeguards made that rare.

Questions:

1. When have you seen something that appeared to be safe actually become deadly?
2. What cults or heresies are you aware of?

Standby

Ed (not his real name) was one of my favorites at a denominational headquarters where I worked for four years. That's why I feel badly that this had to happen to him. Hilarious as it is, the pain was real.

When I hired on, I received permission as part of my employment to travel and stay updated, though travel was rare for editor-types. The only restriction was to get my work done and I would not be subsidized in the travel. I was on my own.

Not to worry. At that time, various airlines offered clergy fares with discounts that reached 50%. The catch? You had to fly standby. No problem. Travel became my game. Using Ozark, Allegheny and Texas International (remember them?) I could fly for what seemed like peanuts to me. I studied the schedules and found the flights most likely to have space. As a result, I was never bumped. I always made my flight. It was fun.

Here, the beauty (smile) of bureaucracy struts down the runway. Word spread around the building about the success of my traveling and finally found its way (it was a struggle) to the offices with carpet on the floor. In typical fashion, the edict came: "Everyone must travel on clergy fares to save money." I might add parenthetically "just like Erwin."

Now let's leave the present moment and go some time later to a regular and infamous coffee break group that included Ed and me. He joined the group one day with his head laying sideways on his shoulder as if sewn there. "Ed, what's going on? Are you doing some heavy thinking and your head is tired?"

"Don't talk to me, Gayle. This is all your fault!"

"My fault? What do you mean?"

"Well, word of your traveling so cheaply reached the bosses and we were all ordered to fly standby on clergy fares. I was on my way to conduct a very important banquet meeting when they bumped me off an airplane about 200 miles away from my destination and just three hours before the banquet was to begin. I had to rent a car and drive more than 100 miles an hour just to get there. The tension was so great in my body that one of my neck muscles tightened up and won't let go. The doctor says I might be this way for weeks."

"Wow, I am truly sorry."

"At least they changed their minds about clergy fares."

"If someone would have bothered to ask me, I would have explained how to fly standby."

"Well, nobody did. It is all past now."

Sure enough, after a couple of weeks, Ed gradually raised his head higher and higher. However, occasionally, at this infamous coffee break gathering, when I saw him coming I would yell, "Hey, Ed. Standby!" And then I would lay my head on my shoulder. Sometimes I wonder about me.

Questions:

1. How has someone tried to copy you with humorous results?
2. Have you ever been blamed for something you had nothing to do with?

Five Times Is Enough

In 1984, I did something for the fifth time at my house that I think should gain me extra respect. I taught the fifth member of my family how to drive. This time it was my son, Clyde. He reached the magical age of 15 when young men's fancies turn toward driving.

We found the largest vacant parking lot in our area and there he began to learn the fine art of gears and...whoomp...clutches...whoomp. After about 30 minutes on the first day, he was ready to go home. I gladly accommodated.

We moved from first gear on succeeding days to second and third gears. Soon, the parking lot was not adequate for us. I said to him, "Clyde, it is time to go out on the street."

"No, Dad."

"Yes, we have to do it."

At first, he drove with my side of the car almost in the ditch. After a while, his comfort zone brought us to the next plateau. "Clyde, it's time to go out on the freeway."

"No, Dad!"

"Yes, Son."

So, he learned to merge and change lanes and otherwise drive as if everyone else was a raving maniac. Time had now come for the ultimate test. In Southern California, the freeway interchange from I-605 South to I-10 East was designed by someone who...well, you have to see it. In just a few feet, two lanes of cars must completely change places. You get cold sweats just thinking about it. But the time had come. "Clyde, we need to merge from I-605 South to I-10 East."

"No, Dad, Please!"

"Yes, Son."

Quiet permeated the car as we drove south. All thoughts concentrated on this ultimate test. As we drove into the interchange, Clyde looked back over his left shoulder to get a glimpse of the last face he ever expected to see. To our delight, the lane was empty. He moved over and whipped out onto I-10 East and moved into a faster lane. Clyde is normally a rather quiet person, but now he could not contain his feelings:

"Thank you, Jesus!" he shouted.

Now on to the DMV, where, with minimal testing they granted his license. Now, we were at home together, mission accomplished. I looked at him and thought, "There is so much yet that you don't know. You don't know what a carburetor does. You don't understand a transmission. You can't comprehend inertia. You have never had this car in a power stop. You have no concept of liability. Our family's finances are in your hands. There is a ticket in your future. Probably an accident."

But even with these thoughts, I reached into my pocket and handed him a set of keys. I admit that my palms were sweating a bit.

Jesus said to a confused Peter and an incompetent apostolic band in Matthew 16, "I give to you the keys to the kingdom...."

Do you suppose he thought, "You have no concept of the kingdom. There is a ticket in your future, probably an accident." Do you suppose his palms were a bit sweaty as he handed over the keys? Nonetheless, he gave them and us the keys.

Questions:

1. If you taught someone how to drive, what pressure did it put on your relationship?
2. Do you feel Jesus has given you the keys to the kingdom, and, if so, how would you say you use them?

In One Month I'll Be Twenty-One

Everyone knows that Chicago, Denver, Atlanta and Dallas are great centers of air travel and major connecting hubs. Another hub is long overdue in credit—Effingham, Illinois. Never heard of it? Not much to hear except it is the O'Hare of bus travel. It holds a permanent spot in my memory, but I am ahead of myself.

My days finished on a denominational staff in Springfield, Missouri, I joined the staff of a church in Urbana, Illinois. Unfortunately, my schedule of other ministry and the sale of our house forced me to complete the move from one city to the other in three days. Our accumulation required two rental trucks. Our new host church had the answer. Bring a one-way truck over, leave it here; we will unload it while you and one of our interns go back by bus. He will help you load another truck which he can drive over for you. Perfect. I couldn't think of a better solution. That was the only way I could complete the move and stay sane.

Loading the first truck with the help of friends, I completed the eight-hour journey to Urbana and turned the truck over to the folks there. The intern assigned to help me (let's call him Mel) and I headed back by bus on an all-night trip. We had to change buses in two places—Effingham and St. Louis.

We arrived in Effingham to connect to St. Louis. Problems unforeseeable awaited us. Their PA system was not working. No signs were posted to indicate connections or times. No parking stalls were numbered. In fact, there were no stalls. Buses merely pulled up to whatever gravel or grass allowed a bus. We used our only option—hunt buses that said "St. Louis" on the marquee. Every attempt to board one of those buses was rebuffed by the driver. We, along with many others confronted the desk people and were told to just wait. OK, except there was no place to wait. I felt like someone wandering by a Jordan River that refused to part.

Finally, rumor reached us as we continued to search for buses arriving, that a bus from storage in the back would go to St. Louis. We rushed back, found the only bus with an open door and entered. Everyone immediately launched into uncontrollable coughing and gagging. The bus had been closed, fumigated and not aired out before we boarded. We all now understood nerve gas.

We sat in the dark and waited uneasily, not truly knowing that this bus would go to St. Louis and wondering if we were missing opportunities back in the main lot of finding an appropriate bus. Finally, a uniformed driver came on the bus, put his name plate over the driver's seat and announced that we were going to St. Louis. His second announcement unnerved me. "I never make this run. I only do Chicago, but they needed a driver and took me off Chicago for this. It's OK. They gave me the directions."

I settled back to get a few winks before St. Louis. Our connection to Springfield was two hours away and it would be tight. Two hours later, I woke up. The bus was parked in a residential neighborhood; the door was open; the driver was gone; but the engine was running. "Mel, where are we? We missed our St. Louis connection. What is going on?"

"You won't believe this, Gayle. We are back in Effingham. We drove for an hour before the driver realized we were lost and retraced his steps back here. He was too embarrassed to drive into the station, so he parked a block away and walked over there."

"You can't be serious!"

"I am."

About then, the driver returned, apologized for the mix-up and explained that they gave him wrong directions before but now he had the correct ones. I wanted to kick myself for not staying awake at the beginning since I knew the way to St. Louis and could have prevented this. We re-began our journey through a wooded ever-decreasing street until we turned onto a narrow gravel road and crossed over a raised railroad—not a good act for a big bus. I quickly shouted to the driver that this was not the way to St. Louis and we must hopefully find a large or circular driveway to turn around, otherwise we were stuck. We did find a large circular driveway at a nightclub. I told the driver that I knew the way to St. Louis and I would help him. He argued a little telling me that this was the direction they gave him. "Trust me," I told him, "this is not the way. No bus like this would ever drive on this kind of road."

He agreed and I led him back to the freeway and we turned toward St. Louis. He said, "I will be OK now. I know the way from here." With not-quite-total relief, I went back to sleep. There were two bridges over the Mississippi River into St. Louis—the free freeway bridge and an old narrow toll bridge that you could exit onto. I expected to wake up pulling into the bus station but awoke as the brakes signaled our exit toward the toll bridge. I shouted again, "Do you know where you are going?" He assured me that he did as we pulled up to the toll gate.

"Fifty cents!" the gatekeeper told him.

"Could I pay you when I come back over?" came the reply.

"Fifty cents!"

"Let me give you an IOU."

"Fifty cents!"

"Can I leave you my driver's license? I don't have any money."

"Fifty cents or this bus isn't moving."

The driver turned and looked helplessly at me. I reached into my pocket and pulled out 50 cents and gave it to him.

Shortly afterward, we arrived in St. Louis. A weary two-hour wait and four-hour ride brought us finally to Springfield. Mel asked me to take him to his old college to visit with his girlfriend while I rented another truck. He didn't seem interested in helping me load but offered to be ready early in the morning to drive back.

I dropped him off and came back to the truck rental place. As I filled out the forms, the agent asked me if I would be driving the truck. I wanted to know why he asked. He informed me that if I was not driving, the driver had to be at least twenty-one years old or he could not rent me the truck. I panicked. Finally, I located someone at the college who knew where Mel's girlfriend lived and helped me get the number. Mel was there.

"Mel, how old are you?"

"In one month I will be twenty-one."

"Are you free to help me load the truck?"

"No. I haven't seen my girlfriend for several weeks and I want to spend the time here."

I don't know what sins of thought I need to confess here. Just pick any you think might apply.

I worked long into the night, alone, loading this second truck, caught a few hours of sleep and went back to pick up Mel at his girlfriend's house for the long return to Urbana and one more return trip to Springfield—this time alone and without my sanity.

Questions:

1. Has there been a time in your life when you worked so hard and so under pressure that you thought you might collapse?
2. When you are tired or frustrated, what weaknesses begin to express themselves in you?

Those Flying Machines

When you approach the two-million-mile mark in flying, stories proliferate. I have many.

A moment never to be forgotten occurred on takeoff from the airport in Harare, Zimbabwe to return to London on a British Airways 747 flight. We had just begun what pilots call "rotation" and our wheels had left the ground when I heard the "Uh Oh!" of a gentleman flying with me.

One of the right-side engines had burst into momentary flame. The pilot sat the plane back down on the runway with a slap and applied the brakes full force. The plane chattered and shook as it roamed back and forth across the runway trying hard with the heaviness of full fuel tanks to stop. I wondered if the plane would come apart. Finally, the plane came to a stop.

For minutes, the passengers sat in stunned silence before the pilot came on and said, "Folks, as you can see, we have had a problem. Everything is red hot and we need to just sit here and cool off. Our tires are all flat and our brakes are glowing. Fortunately, we are on the second longest runway in the world and we are 50 feet from the end. We are lucky." I knew luck had nothing to do with it.

A family on the plane who knew I was a minister said they felt the plane had been saved because I was on board. I assured them that was poor theology. Nonetheless, they insisted on knowing which flight I would later take to London, because they wanted to take the same one. The only real disadvantage of the delayed flight was that it canceled my trip on to Ireland and consequently delayed my first journey there by 15 years.

∽

So accustomed to flying, I rarely even notice when the plane actually takes off. At some point, I become aware, of course, but just minutes into this flight out of the old Denver Stapleton airport, I knew something was funny. We had flown long enough for me to notice and when I looked out the window, I saw that we had not gained much altitude at all. We also seemed to be doing excessive turning. I waited for what I knew would be the inevitable statement from the pilot. I didn't have to wait very long.

"Ladies and Gentlemen, we had something happen as we took off and we have lost hydraulic power. We don't want you to be alarmed but this does have some seriousness to it. (Ha!) They have shut down the airport waiting for our return. As we land, you will see emergency equipment lined up along the runway. Hopefully, we will come to a safe stop, although we cannot do any steering."

We landed safely and waited a long time after being towed off the runway while the experts examined to see what had happened. Finally, the pilot assured those who had dogs or other animals in the luggage compartment that they had been taken off and put in a cooler and safe place. At that announcement, all the people in the plane began barking.

⌒

The distance from Toronto to Philadelphia is short by air, but being on United, I had to go through Chicago to get there. Not too bad. Just two one-hour flights. Or so I thought.

As we approached Chicago, we crossed over a major storm line. You tend to notice those. We circled Chicago for a long time before the captain informed us that landing conditions were unacceptable and we would fly to Indianapolis to refuel. Short flight, except that we recrossed that heavy storm line. A few jaws clinched. We landed, refueled and returned to Chicago; however, we crossed, once again, that heavy storm line, or better—lurched across the line.

As we descended and lowered our wheels, we broke through the clouds into an eerie scene, one I had never observed before. The plane began to act in ways that tightened my jaw. Suddenly, the wheels came up and if a plane can "scratch off," this plane did. We climbed as fast as we could. About the time I thought we would go into orbit, the captain informed us that we had hit a wind shear and we had to take emergency measures. But now, we did not have enough fuel to circle the airport, so we needed to go back to Indianapolis to refuel. Once again, we crossed the storm line. For the first time in all my flying, I saw attendants going up and down the aisle handing out barf bags.

We landed in Indianapolis and pulled off the runway, stopped and waited and waited. Again the captain came on. "Folks, I have good news and bad news." (Oh, how I love that statement!) "The good news is that we have landed at Indianapolis. The bad news is that so has everybody else. We have no idea when we can get to a gate."

The "no idea" that became a reality was four hours. When we finally pulled up to the terminal, I had been on that plane for eight hours on what was supposed to be a one-hour flight and crossed a major storm line four times. I had already missed speaking that night at a men's retreat, and I didn't want to go back to Chicago. Mercifully, they put me on a flight straight to Philadelphia the next morning.

Questions:

1. Describe your main fear in traveling.
2. Share your airplane or travel stories.

Jake Moments

Jake was a mean logger whose dramatic conversion I observed as a small child caused me to call subsequent dramatic moments of encountering God "Jake Moments." In my first book of stories, **That Reminds Me of a Story***, I detailed that conversion as well as others. The work of God goes on. Here are only a few of the abounding Jake stories I continue to observe.*

∽

The leather jacket, the chains, the rings in every part of the visible body caught my attention. Who knows what kind of thoughts brought that about. Desire for attention? Expression of self? Rebellion? Fitting in with his crowd? Who knows? But here he walked. I didn't notice his family following him at a discreet distance, but when he entered the water and his family cried unashamedly, I noticed everything and turned away to hide my own tears.

This occurred at Applegate Christian Fellowship led by Pastor Jon Courson and located in Southern Oregon. Their summertime outdoor amphitheater meetings permit all the congregation together at once, though their growth is making even that prospect dimmer.

At the close of those Sunday morning services, the response to the call is usually massive and is followed by baptism in a creek-like baptistry. Courson often spends hours baptizing and praying with the people who come. My emotions overflow as I watch young and old, families and individuals who come. When God wins, he wins big!

↜

Beside the swimming pool of a large vacation center that was built to house the "Young Pioneers," the youth indoctrination program of the communist regime in Hungary, I watched as something new and glorious happened in that country. In the blossoming of their freedom, young people were turning to God and sealing that new relationship in a great baptismal service. In spite of the drizzle adding a slight unpleasantness to the surroundings, joy reigned. At one point, I could restrain my tears no longer. A young married couple, now serving the Lord together walked into the pool and their pastor, Greg Opean, baptized them together. I heard the applause but could barely see the hugs through the tears.

On the final night of the gathering, as I closed the message, two young people responded to the invitation—a young man and a young woman. After a later communion service, I returned to my bungalow to prepare for leaving the following day. As I and four others sat in semi-darkness because of an electrical failure, the young man who had responded made his way haltingly up the porch steps and tapped on our door. We invited him in and as he choked back tears told us in Hungarian how thankful he was for what had happened. He had been deeply moved and was so very glad now that he knew the Lord. I and the Lord had a good talk afterward.

↩

Back when Zimbabwe was still Rhodesia and the civil war raged, guerrilla fighters had driven farmers out of the northeast highlands. One farmer, a man I befriended while there told me about his conversion. Having been driven off his farm, he could only wait and hope to return. However, in a fit of defiance, he decided to return and fish in his lake. He and a worker drove to the farm. Then the farmer got in the back of the pickup to watch for any military activity as the worker drove toward the lake.

Unfortunately, they hit a land mine in the road. As he related it to me, he went up into the air as a sinner and came back down as a Christian.

↩

Few things touch me more than to see homes built or restored. In a California church at the close of the second Sunday morning service, a drama unfolded that I missed but someone in tears told me later. As people streamed toward the front in response to a call to salvation, unknown to me, an older divorced couple sat on opposite ends of the curved balcony from each other. They were also unaware of each other's presence. Nor were they aware that the other was responding to the call to repentance. From those opposite sides, they met each other at the front and fell into each other's arms as they also fell into the arms of God.

～

It was the third morning service at Ft. Lauderdale. This morning, something most unusual happened that left me melting before God. The stream of seekers began, somewhat to my surprise, but this was different. Within seconds I realized that it was almost exclusively couples walking arm in arm or even walking in embrace toward the front. I knew that new homes were beginning at that moment, repair was occurring, sins were forgotten, forgiveness was flowing.

～

"Do you remember me?" That kind of question creates high tension in me as I search my memory. The question came from a smiling lady after service at Harvest Christian Fellowship in Riverside, California. Yes, her face was familiar, but I had to plead ignorance. She continued. "A year ago in Atchison, Kansas I asked you to pray for my husband to be saved. We prayed and you also recommended some of your tapes that would help him understand God. When I got home, we had a six-hour Gayle Erwin listening session and...."

She turned and pointed to someone standing a few feet behind her. I hadn't noticed him, but now her husband walked up to me with a beaming face and arms outstretched for a hug. He had come to know the Lord as a result and they wanted me to know. A home was now complete. I must have looked funny smiling so big and crying at the same time.

My life for God began as a child. Though this means I do not have a dramatic testimony, I am grateful beyond words for the remorse God prevented by this early decision and also by the increased amount of learning available to me because of my upbringing in a thoroughly Christian home. When I see children respond I want to grab each one and hug them welcoming them into the kingdom. Some (depending on age) might be embarrassed by that. In some cases I simply observe and exult at what I see.

Jacobs are being turned into Israels all over the world.

Questions:

1. For whose conversion are you currently praying?
2. Whose conversion (other than your own) has meant the most to you?

The Evangelist

My father's injury and disability brought us to a relationship with almost all of the famous tent evangelists who populated the 1950s. Because of their emphasis on healing and our own desperation for healing, we traveled to wherever they were. Names included Oral Roberts, Gayle Jackson, Jack Coe and A. A. Allen. They each had the world's largest tent. And they were big, seating around 10,000 people. This story about Jack Coe begins when I was about five years old.

My parents had started a church in Pascagoula, Mississippi about 1940 in the early days of World War II. Military installations dotted the coast, but the largest one was Keesler Air Force Base in Biloxi, Mississippi. We often had visitors come from there.

One tall gangly visitor joined me in the front of our church property where I practiced the universal activity of little boys—throwing rocks. After a brief conversation, he picked up a rock and actually threw it over the tall pine trees that surrounded us. I could not believe what I saw. I handed him another rock and asked him to do it again. He obliged. Finally, his begging for relief exceeded my begging for him to throw, and he went inside leaving me with memories of olympic (to me) rock throwing.

Forty years later I learned that the visitor was Jack Coe, who had just become a Christian and whose zeal in his new relationship brought him into conflict with military expectations. He came to my parents for fellowship and comfort through his trials.

My second encounter with him was not so direct and personal. My early teens coincided with the height of the tent revival season. By then, we knew and followed, to some degree, the schedules of them all. Unfortunately, living in Greenwood, Mississippi tended to be a bit off their normal path. However, an interesting side effect of the tent revival phenomenon had a semi-tragic humor to it.

The guys with the big tents could be called the "major leaguers." They attracted the largest crowds and the most press attention. Frankly, some of what they did was awe-inspiring, while other activities reeked of manipulation and fraud. But I digress. Each of the majors had certain readily identifiable quirks that set them apart from the others. Oral Roberts, for instance, claimed a certain feeling in his right hand when he thought there would be healing. A. A. Allen claimed oil dripping from his hands; William Branham claimed a halo. Gayle Jackson seemed to be the one intent on teaching while emphasizing the Baptism of the Holy Spirit. Jack Coe? Well...Jack had a strange approach that I even hesitate to express. When he would pray for people for healing, he often would ask them where they hurt, tell them to raise their hands and close their eyes, and then would hit them where they hurt as he began his prayer. God let him get away with it and people were actually healed.

These major leaguers spawned minor leaguers, men whose tents were not so large or whose press coverage not so extensive. The minor leaguers sought to attach themselves to the success of the majors by adopting the idiosyncrasies of the evangelist they felt to be most successful.

∽

A Jack Coe clone came to town. He set up what must have been the largest tent in our county. He seemed intrigued by the fist of Jack Coe. One night, when people were coming across the platform to be prayed for, he asked one brother where he hurt. "My stomach," came the reply. He then instructed to close his eyes and raise his hands. The clone then hit him in the stomach. The man was not healed, but he was knocked unconscious.

When consciousness returned, the unhealed man was also not fooled. Now the unfooled fist did not ask where the evangelist hurt, only where he would like to hurt; and the evangelist was now unconscious. By the next morning, the tent and the evangelist had disappeared.

∽

My grandparents seemed to be ahead of the game on technological developments. They had a TV set as soon as they were practical.

However, in some church circles, TV was the ultimate enemy and many preachers abandoned the hunt for the "roaring lion" and turned their attention to "rabbit ears." Jack Coe was one of them. He called it "hellivision." He graphically described it as the devil's tail sticking up from your roof and leading right down into your living room. I am inclined to believe him more in this day.

Once, when Coe was conducting a crusade in the hometown of my grandparents, they invited him to a lunch at their home. He accepted.

This sent my grandmother into an ethical tizzy. They had a large TV right in the middle of their living room. She insisted that my grandfather take it away before Coe came to visit. He refused, saying that it would be hypocritical. Daily, she insisted; daily, he refused.

However, my resourceful grandmother figured out what to do. When Coe arrived, much to the humor of my grandfather, the TV set was appropriately fully covered with a sheet so he wouldn't "see" it. Grandpa laughed and said, "Ma, he can't miss it now."

⌒

The 1950s were Communist hunting, Joe McCarthy days. Everyone talked of spies and treason. Radio evangelists raised more money to fight Communists than to preach the Gospel. Coe got in on the wave. He promised that on a certain night in his big tent, he would reveal the biggest Communist in the USA. You must have a ticket to get in that night. The tickets were free but Coe expressed that he hoped you would use discretion in giving them away.

Although I was skeptical, as an early teenager, that Coe would have any sort of access to such information, it seemed like good theater, so I was there. The message was weak, but at least it was long. He masterfully delayed the revelation until after the offering had been taken and the sermon had reached a prolonged conclusion. Actually, the sermon and revelation were totally unrelated. I struggled all evening to make the connection.

Finally, the revelation came, almost as a side and after thought. The biggest Communist in the USA was Kate Smith, the famous "God Bless America" singer. I can't even remember what I thought, other than disbelief, when it was over. I guess you have to be careful what you sing.

Questions:

1. What experiences have you had with what might be called "revival"?
2. Can you describe any manipulation you felt from religious leaders?

What Will Two Dollars Get?

Recall the story of the lady whose groom came in out of the field in overalls to get married? Here is the rest of that story.

Every month, I published a small newsletter for the people of the church and passed it out in service and mailed it to those who were absent. Every time this lady received her newsletter, she would write a letter in response giving her own personal news to me. Each letter from her would contain a prayer request and would have a dollar bill hand sewn into the letter.

One letter seemed urgent. Along with the dollar bill came this request: "Please pray for rain. If we don't get rain this week, we will lose our crop and I cannot afford that." Frankly, I don't remember any details about my prayer, but that week, we had the ideal rain, taking almost the whole week to deliver an inch of rain.

I paid little attention until about ten days later, I received another letter from the lady. This one thanked me for praying for the rain; however, rather than the usual dollar bill, two dollars were sewn to the letter. The prayer request this time was, "Pray that God will resurrect my old husband. I don't like this new one. He won't take me to church."

I suppose that she thought that if a dollar brought rain, perhaps two dollars would get a resurrection.

Questions:

1. What do you expect from God because of your generosity and faithfulness in giving?
2. What do you think my own reaction would have been if she had sewn a check for one million dollars to the letter?

Killer Faith

I opened my morning paper and quickly scanned the headlines. The typical news portrayed a troubled world, but one headline troubled my world. I didn't want to read the article, but I knew I had to. The headline read, "Faith Kills Boy." I later discovered it was on front pages around the nation.

The article related the story of a couple whose small son suffered from diabetes and needed frequent medication. At a church service, an itinerant preacher prayed for the boy and declared him healed. The parents were informed that they no longer needed to provide medicine. In faith, they withheld his medicine and the boy died. Fellow church members urged the father to claim the resurrection of his son. For several days they lived in a combined state of expectancy and denial.

Finally, with the police involved, the couple was charged with manslaughter. Both of them were convicted.

When I read the article, I could not know that just a few years later, this couple would submit an article to a magazine I published. The manuscript, entitled, "Some Things I Learned from Watching My Son Die," detailed several items of new maturity, two of which stand out in my mind.

"First," they stated, "we learned that God is a God of reality. When He heals, He heals. If He doesn't, He doesn't. Either can be verified."

I thought of all the misery they suffered in "claiming by faith" the life of their son. They had been taught that if they used the right words and never made any sort of "negative" statement (regardless of realities) then their claims would come about.

My mind drove that theology to its absurdity. Suppose, for instance, one of my grandchildren asked me for an ice cream cone. The odds are very good that they would get it. (I might get one, too.) However, I would never instruct them to hold their hand as if they actually had a cone in it and lick the air all the while proclaiming its good taste, and then, if they faithfully did so throughout the day, I might give them an ice cream cone. I would never do that to them.

Second, the couple learned that love is greater than faith. "We acted in faith toward our son, but we did not act in love and love is greater than faith" (1 Cor. 13:13). These words rang in my ears. How totally obvious and yet how totally unnoticed that statement from Scripture.

Questions:

1. Have you ever believed something and later wished you hadn't?
2. In what ways have you been religiously manipulated?

Mare and Colt

The pastor asked if I minded stopping by a horse corral with him to feed a parishioner's horse before we headed for the Sunday morning service. He explained to me that the parishioner was on vacation and would be back in a few days. I assured him that I not only didn't mind but, being a horse lover, would enjoy the stop on the way to church.

He gathered the feed and went to do his regular chore as I walked along with him. This time was different from other feeding times. The horse skittered back and forth and seemed unwilling to take food from the pastor. With mounting frustration, the pastor sought to resolve the problem, speaking as comfortingly to the horse as he could.

Finally, he turned to me and said, "I don't understand this. This horse has never done this before. Perhaps she is bothered by your presence."

I admitted that could possibly be true, though horses are rarely that discriminating when it comes to food. I offered another solution. "I think that if you will move away from between that horse and her colt, she will calm down."

Realization covered his face, closely followed by sheepishness. He moved to the side, and immediately the horse became manageable.

I thought of how often I accidentally got between my congregation and their Lord and couldn't understand why they were so unmanageable. My job is to just get out of their way and feed them.

Questions:

1. What actions or statements have you heard that make God seem more distant to you?
2. What do you do to make it easy for people to approach God or believe in him?

Mr. Clean

At a certain Christian college, the president of the student body this particular year could only be described as "Mr. Clean." He was so straight and straightforward that no one believed that he had ever imagined sin. As it happened this particular semester, the roommate assigned to him in the dormitory could only be described as "Mr. Dirty." If anyone prayed much, it was for the salvation of Mr. Dirty.

During the course of the semester and during a time of spiritual intensity, wonderful things happened and Mr. Dirty had his encounter with God. The place was ecstatic. Now, campus tradition mandated a celebration. When the hand of God moved so greatly, they would have a giant bonfire to celebrate what God had done. They gathered around the fire to worship, and, perhaps, write their sins on a piece of paper and throw it into the fire as an act of repentance and forgiveness. In fact, if there was some thing that they felt had separated them from God, they could throw that into the fire.

Mr. Dirty had something to throw away. His extensive collection of pornography, now deemed unnecessary, headed to the fire. One problem. Mr. Dirty had a job on that night and could not be there personally to throw the pornography away, so he asked his roommate, Mr. Clean, to throw it away for him.

Now, you need to see this scene in your mind. Here are a thousand students gathered around the fire. The spiritual temperature is as hot as the fire. Then, here comes Mr. Clean, the president of the student body with his arms full of this trash. As he made his way through the outer edges of the crowd, others would look at his armful and exclaim, "Oh, I didn't know." And the buzz would begin around the circle—whisper to ear, whisper to ear. The sweat began to flow from the brow of Mr. Clean.

As he made his way through the more tightly packed crowd near the fire, those around would look down at his armful and remark, "Oh, I didn't know." The inner circle whisper began. By the time he reached the fire, sweat poured from his forehead, and every eye fixed on him.

Mr. Clean looked around, threw a magazine into the fire. The crowd cheered. Mr. Clean exclaimed for all to hear, "It's not mine! It's not mine!"

He threw another in the fire. The crowd cheered again. Again, he shouted, "It's not mine! It's not mine!" Would you say he was uncomfortable?

I realized that when Jesus hung on the cross, he had every ounce of my sin and crud (and yours) hanging on him and never once did he proclaim, "It's not mine!"

Questions:

1. If you were Mr. Dirty's roommate, would you be able to throw his pornography away so publicly? What alternatives might you suggest?
2. What does "Jesus dying for our sins" mean to you?

The Secret Agent

*Seeing Jesus clearly, as I discovered and explained in the book **The Jesus Style**, changes absolutely everything in your life for which you become profoundly grateful. The major change area is in how you view people. Once you understand the great love and grace of God toward yourself, sheer gratitude pushes you to be loving and merciful to others. Prejudices crumble. Differences fade. Relationships grow.*

A major test of this view of Jesus came in 1978 in Africa. I was invited to teach at an interracial renewal conference.

Anxious about delivering my message on the servanthood Nature of Jesus in a different culture, I pre-preached it to one of my black students from East Africa. He informed me that they would love it and that I would be the first white man they had ever heard say that. I also determined to be "with" each of the races at the conference.

I shared, in my normal strange humorous style, the traits of Jesus and spent rewarding amounts of time among the blacks there, hearing their stories, eating with them, getting to know their colorful names, learning words and phrases in their Shona language, visiting their offices, praying for them, having them pray for me, having my eyes opened.

On the last day of the conference, one of the white brethren, whom I had come to know and saw frequently, approached me after one of my visits with a young black man and pulled me aside to talk with me. "I am going to tell you something that you are not supposed to know," he began. "I am a member of the Secret Service of the government and I have been assigned to watch you. I want you to know that if our people had treated the blacks the way you have been treating them, we would never have had a civil war."

He walked away and I stood there stunned. What I had done was merely a natural outflow of the nature of Jesus. Though I should have been highly affirmed, I became deeply sorrowful, even depressed, that this had not been the natural process of the church.

Questions:

1. What experience have you had where you thought you were doing one thing and discovered that you had accomplished something else?
2. If you have read *The Jesus Style*, in what ways have you noticed that you adopted the Nature of Jesus?

Parts is Parts

In the letter to the Church at Colossi, Paul writes that Jesus is the "head of the body, the church." That realization clarified something for me. It also caused me to come up with a saying that I think will make me famous: "If you see a body without a head, it's dead!" Remember that you heard it here first.

The sadness of it all is that if you were to attend all of the churches in any given city on any given Sunday, you would discover that some death is there. This grieves me, but the problem is simply that they have chosen to separate themselves from Jesus either in attitude or action. Perhaps they even doubt his existence. They certainly don't consult him. They are a body separated from the head.

That also reminded me of a rather gross (you don't have to read this) story. I am an old farm boy. We farm kids know that chickens don't grow up inside plastic bags with weights and prices written on them. Whenever my grandmother needed to feed the farm hands, she lacked the luxury of a quick trip to the grocery store; that was a once-a-month all-day affair. She simply walked to the chicken yard, and, with a special hooked stick, grabbed a fryer by the leg and pulled it out.

Then the grossest thing would happen. She took the chicken by the head and began to whirl the body around and around until the body flew off and the head remained in her hands. (I told you this was gross.) For the next few minutes, that chicken was the most active it had ever been in its life. Flop, flop, flop, run, run, run, flop, flop.

An untrained observer might conclude, "What a live chicken!" But the fact is, that chicken was dead. It had been separated from its head. Sometimes, churches that are dead vote to increase their activities. Flop, flop, flop, run, run, run, flop, flop. An untrained observer might conclude, "What a live church!" but the fact is, that church is dead. It has been separated from its head.

Jesus is the head of the body!

Questions:

1. Describe some unusual actions of your grandparents.
2. What rituals of the past have disappeared from your life?

Ruined Weekend

The plane, full of party-types, whooped it up on the way to Las Vegas. For some reason, they took up with me and I whooped with them. As the activity died down, I got up to go to the back of the plane. The ringleader of the party group spotted me and called me over.

"Hey, Mister. Just what do you do?"

I gave my ready answer: "I have more fun than anybody in the world."

"I believe that," he spouted.

"I go all over the world teaching on the Nature of Jesus."

He slapped his hand to his forehead and exclaimed, "Oh, my god. You just ruined my weekend."

"Me? What did I do?"

"You just said that word, 'Jesus'. Now I have to think about this."

"Just saying that ruined your weekend?"

"Yes, I'm on my way to Las Vegas. I'm looking for women. Now, I am going to have to think about this because you said that word, 'Jesus'."

"Awww. Too bad."

I did not sorrow over ruining his weekend, but I did have a brief opportunity to share the Gospel.

Questions:

1. What have you observed happening when you say the word "Jesus" to someone you don't know?
2. If someone observed you in a crowd for thirty minutes, how do you think they would describe you?

Sshh, It's a Secret

Secret Societies

Secret Societies trouble me for several reasons. The fact that Jesus was light and in him was no darkness at all seems incompatible with membership in something secret. The fact that Jesus said men love darkness rather than light because their deeds are evil lays a severe indictment on secret societies.

This is why I avoided fraternities when I was in college. (I didn't avoid sororities quite as much.) However, I was inducted into an honorary fraternity while I was in college. I don't remember the name exactly, *eata bitta pi* or something like that. And I'm not sure why I was chosen except that I did not blow up the chemistry lab.

On the night when I was to be brought into membership, they ushered me and others into a candle-lit room. Now I am always suspicious when I am in a candle-lit room. I usually think that this is going to cost me something. Even when my wife cooks a wonderful meal and we eat by candle light, I enjoy it but always feel just a twinge of suspicion that this is going to cost me something. At any rate, they brought us into this candle-lit room for the induction ceremony.

To my surprise, the leader in the course of the evening announced, "And now, the secrets known only to the members of this fraternity."

I thought, "Oh, brother! This is not supposed to be that kind of society." When he finished relating them, I almost laughed. I thought, "Don't worry. Those secrets are safe with me."

The secrets were no more profound than saying "Circles are round and squares have corners on the edges."

Living in the light still beats secrecy.

Secrecy in the Church

With a group of highly skilled academic men, I shared in founding a magazine. The purpose was to provide a forum for theological subjects to be discussed in an unofficial manner within a certain denomination. These men, whose lives had been on the frontline of church planting, missions and teaching, had managed to be spared the realities of denominational politics (which I had, on the other hand, been in position to observe intimately) and were most surprised at the extremely hostile response on the part of officials to the magazine.

The founding of our magazine coincided with revelations by a national columnist of some questionable financial activity on the part of the top person in the denomination. The resultant charade of political action caused us to propose a "sunshine resolution" similar to the Freedom of Information Act of the federal government that would permit access by any ordained minister of the denomination to the minutes of any meeting of the denomination from committees on up except for those of discipline that would compromise an individual's privacy.

Now, one would think that a biblically oriented organization would immediately see the light of that call and back it fully. Such was not the case. Secrecy reigned stronger in the denomination than in the Pentagon. Twenty-eight of us involved in the magazine were summarily removed from the denomination without hearing or notification. We were reinstated even before we knew we had been excluded as some cooler heads prevailed. I am writing something that, to this day, has never been revealed. Secrecy still reigns.

However, darkness is sought only for one reason.

Questions:

1. When you try to keep a secret, what effect does it have on you?
2. What does "walking in the light" mean to you?

Shell Top Camper

I understand this story to be true and that it happened to some people I know. I am not about to check it out.

Many years of pastoring the same church resulted in a whole month of vacation every year for the pastor and his wife. Their favorite form of vacation was camping in a pickup with a camper shell. One particular year, as they neared the end of another joyous rest and they made their way home, they found themselves further away on Saturday night than they planned. It would be necessary for them to drive all night to be back in time for him to preach the next morning.

As the journey droned on, the pastor finally said to his wife, "I can't do it. I am already sleepy and it isn't safe for me to continue driving."

She responded, "But we have to continue on. You are expected back in the morning." He drove a while longer and finally gave up. All was not lost.

His wife said, "I am not sleepy. Let me drive. You can get in the back of the camper and go to sleep while I drive."

Excellent idea. They stopped. He got out and walked back and into the camper, took off all his clothes except his shorts and settled into a deep sleep while his wife drove.

After a couple of hours, she became a little drowsy herself and almost missed a stop sign on a lonely wilderness stretch of road. In fact, she had to put the pickup into a power stop that caused it to shudder rather violently to a stop. She hoped that it didn't wake up her husband in the back; however, he woke with a start and immediately thought, "Oh no, we've had a wreck."

He quickly, but groggily, stumbled out the back of the camper to look around and see what she had hit. At that moment, his wife had regained her composure and sped off into the dark wilderness. He ran and yelled to no avail.

Now, here he was dressed only in his shorts beside this almost deserted road in the middle of the night. As the occasional car passed, he would try to flag a ride, but they would only speed up. Finally, a highway patrolman drove along, stopped and asked just what was he doing beside the road dressed only in his shorts.

"Well, I am a pastor and...."

"Sure you are! Here, breathe into this balloon and walk this line."

Finally, sobriety at least proved, they took him to the station and a quick phone call to one of his elders at the church verified to the police that this was, indeed, the pastor of their church. After all the chuckles, clothes were provided and money loaned to charter a light plane to fly him on home.

One problem: He got home before his wife and didn't have a key to get in, so he sat on the front steps to wait for her. Sure enough, just before dawn, the headlights of the pickup turned onto their street. As she turned into the driveway, the light fell on her husband and she was so shocked that she hit the accelerator rather than the brake and demolished the garage.

End of story. However, I often wonder what went through the mind of the elder who knew the story and whether he was able to keep a straight face as his pastor spoke that morning.

Questions:

1. What parts of this story would you have the most trouble believing?
2. What are some funny things you have observed about your pastor?

Tender Ears

Louisiana suffers from the highest illiteracy rate in the nation. That made literature evangelism somewhat wasteful at my first pastorate in Venice, Louisiana. The state legislature, which is known for...ah, well (let's not explore that subject), decided to deal with that problem. They spent quite a sum of money putting up billboards across the state that read, "If you are illiterate and want help, call the following number...."

Now, illiterate people are not lesser people, they simply can't read. I learned some wonderful lessons from some who were "reading challenged." Love and wisdom are not always products of literacy.

⌐

In a state other than Louisiana, a fifty-year-old widower was courting a lady of his age who lived in a big city about seventy-five miles away. They faithfully wrote each other every few days. What she didn't know was that this widower could not read or write. However, he had a trusted friend who would read the lady's letters to him and return the dictated replies.

Once, when his trusted friend was away on vacation, a letter arrived from the city lady. What was he to do? His friend was gone and no one was available to read the letter to him. No one was available, that is, except for a twelve-year-old nephew. The problem? This letter contained things that a twelve-year-old's ears should not hear. What to do? Ah, no problem!

He simply covered the nephew's ears while he read the letter!

You write the questions for this one!

The Funeral

The constant gnawing, foreboding feeling forced me into the most difficult situation. I must tell my wife that, for reasons I cannot explain, I feel that we should forego an after-Christmas trip to see her mother. To my great relief, she expressed the same feelings. The gathering storm was invisible to us.

The Sunday after Christmas showed its predictable blandness, that is, until the evening service. I arrived after the doors opened to see a family of five standing in the foyer with an arriving congregation gathered around them. I watched and listened fascinated as Jesus shined out of all they said and did. When I met them and learned more, I was jealous that they lived 800 miles away.

They were visiting his parents in our town and hesitated to come to our service because he heard that we dressed very fine. I winced at that reputation though the church had the best location in town. At my probing, I learned that the commitment of the family was real with all of them soulwinners. He, a former bomber pilot, had rented a plane and flown to our city with his family. They planned to return the next day, Monday morning.

Though their presence brightened our day, Monday returned me to routine and I let the memory slip away. Tuesday's paper carried a small two-inch item indicating that a small plane was missing, but I made no connection. Wednesday's article, a larger one, arrested me. I knew this was the family. By Thursday, when hope was abandoned, I immediately found the parents and sought to assist them if they needed me. They had been without a pastor for nine months and clung to my offer.

On Saturday, the plane was found in a thick forest. He had lost his way in a major storm and run out of fuel. All were dead. I stayed with the parents assuming the burial would be 800 miles away, but then discovered they would be buried locally. His pastor planned to come over for the memorial service.

Now, new information. The family owned a dry cleaning plant that had prospered, but they chose to live a simple lifestyle to free funds and time for missions activity. At Christmas, they drew names and presented gifts to each other in a unique way. Each person described to the gift receiver what they planned to give but rather than the gift, only the thought was given while the money was put into a jar for a missions trip. Before Christmas, they would take the money as well as abandoned clothes at their plant down to Mexico and spend a week of friendship and evangelism.

You might think them morose over this, but quite the opposite. They were a happy, active, water skiing type of family. Now they were gone.

Another bit of information shook my world. The father of the wife was a wealthy, hostile, Christianity-hating person who despised his son-in-law and openly hoped to see him someday crawling to him for a job. His hostility toward the son-in-law and his pentecostal church exploded as the funeral approached. He refused to let that pentecostal pastor have anything to do with his daughter's funeral. Now, the arrangements fell back to a decision by the son's parents. They asked me if I would do the ceremony. I accepted, smiling at the humor of it all.

At the visitation times in the funeral home, the in-laws never spoke to me personally which was fine with me. However, they brought their lawyer with them and he relayed any messages to me they desired. The main message was, "Keep it short." I smiled and said I would consider it. I knew that I was free to do whatever I wanted.

At the visitation, I learned even more. This son I would be burying was so highly esteemed, that, as one person related, "If he told me that building across the street was going to jump three feet into the air, I would begin staring, because it certainly would." Five people sought me out during the visitation time to ask me how to become a Christian. Each seeker described the loss of such a man and family as so unthinkable that they wanted to be a Christian to help replace them. I long since abandoned any attempt to answer the question, "Why?"

At the funeral service, I detailed the ways the family had stored their treasure in heaven where moth and rust and corruption could not reach. At one point during my sermon, the father-in-law and his daughter who hung fawningly on him at all times, looked up at me and shouted, "Would you shut up!"

As the five hearses carried the bodies to their final resting place, I pondered the hostile misery of the living father-in-law contrasted with the benevolent peacefulness of the buried son and wondered at a justice that someday I would understand.

Questions:

1. Who do you know that you would consider to have died an untimely death?
2. If you have had any friends or relatives who died, what are some things about them that you miss?

The Men's Choir

The Northeast of the United States, much like continental Europe, moved away from its Christian history. Evangelical churches have been difficult to start in that area and tend to remain small with few exceptions. So, it was with great joy that I watched a real Bible teaching church get started and grow steadily on the outskirts of Boston.

As the church grew in the number of men, they asked me to come and conduct a men's retreat (something I commonly do) and I gladly obliged. At the retreat which occurred on Cape Cod, one of the men suggested that they take some time to practice a few of the favorite worship songs and, when they returned, lead the worship service on the following Sunday night. This was a big event, the first time the church had planned to meet on Sunday night.

There was a little hesitancy because of their feelings of inadequacy, but the plans progressed; and, frankly, as I listened to their practice, I wasn't sure practice was going to help them. But they persisted.

When Sunday night arrived and the service began, much to the surprise of the people, the men made their way to the platform to lead the worship service. They even asked me to get in on the act. However, it almost didn't happen.

When the wives saw their husbands doing something they, in their wildest dreams, never thought would happen, when they saw them assuming spiritual leadership, when they saw them actually up front worshipping God, they lost it. Sobs of joy came from every corner of that auditorium. You can finish this, can't you?

These men, seeing their wives weep, were overwhelmed by the power of the event and barely scratched out songs between their own sobs. I wept unashamedly.

Questions:

1. When have you seen such a spiritual victory that it caused you to weep?
2. What, if anything, touches you so deeply that you can't successfully participate without crying?

Jesse

He owned the house where I was born. In fact, he owned the house where my father was born on the same farm. In further fact, the same doctor that traveled 23 miles to deliver my father traveled the same distance to deliver me about 23 years later. Jesse's house and farm carry more warm memories than any spot of my childhood. I risked life and limb climbing to the peak of his barns by gripping the edge of tin roofing sheets. His hogs lost unknown pounds of weight because of running to the slop trough at the sound of my hog-calling practice. The Oklahoma plains became exciting scenery as I climbed to the top of his windmills.

His cattle-watering tanks served as swimming pools though I had to push the occasional pond scum aside. His tractors and combine merited hours of "just riding along" to be with him. In his battered pickup (I helped batter it) I rode shotgun and watched the cattle come running when we entered the pasture. That pickup meant food.

The horse he provided me was beautiful and gentle. I thought it was mine, but I found out that a lot of my cousins thought the horse was theirs. OK. I was free to saddle the horse at age seven and ride him anywhere I wanted. As a city dweller now, I find the next statement very hard to believe myself, but his wife (my grandmother) would make a lunch for me and I would ride down to the river bottom with a rifle and a box of 22s and stay until the box was empty. I had only one caveat—don't shoot any of the cows or horses or any deer, or, as it was strongly hinted, anything alive.

I helped him spread fodder as he ground it and blew it into silos. I ate, and I mean really ate, at his table. I can still smell the bread baking—and the slop bucket kept just outside the kitchen door—nothing was wasted. I used his outhouse (two-holer) 40 yards out at the back of the chicken yard. I probably need therapy from the visits to that outhouse at 20-below-zero temperatures.

I remember his phone, a wall-hanging box with a tube sticking out and a handle on the side that, when vigorously spun in certain code lengths, would produce a person speaking on the other end. I marveled that the wires supporting the phone system were often simple fence wires grafted into the flow. I discovered that there was no such thing as a private line.

I was impressed that, way ahead of others, he had constructed a "wind charger," a generator that captured power from Oklahoma winds (plentiful) and stored the electricity in a garage filled with batteries to provide real and better light than the dangerous kerosene lamps. When the "highline" came, he was already wired and ready. He rigged up a water tank that provided running water for his house and then (whee) brought the toilet indoors. I knew he could do anything. I would drift off to sleep at night to the sound of coyotes howling and awaken to the crowing of roosters.

His workshop had no lock (to his misfortune) so I spent many hours there testing different tools in ways they were not designed. Spinning the blower on his forge provided endless hours of mindless fun. Life could get no better. Ah, but it certainly could get worse. School meant a long bus ride since only about one house occupied each square mile of land. Classrooms became places for me to daydream and sleep and be punished. The farm was much more enticing.

Time and tides ended his farm days and he and my grandmother moved to "the city." There, many years after I had left the farm, I reentered their lives in a way most beneficial to me. I lived with them for an extended period of time as I finished junior high school. The hours I spent at his feet in Bible study are priceless.

A footnote: In 1999, while teaching at the Billy Graham Training Center (The Cove) in Asheville, North Carolina, I met a granddaughter of Dr. Leachman who delivered me. Her name is Gayle. Hmmm.

Questions:

1. What are some of the warmest memories you have of your grandparents?
2. In what ways do you feel your grandparents influenced you? If you don't remember your grandparents, how would you describe the grandfather you would like to have?

The Torch

In 1984 when the Olympic Games came to Los Angeles, one of the gimmicks used to create interest was a torch run across the United States. Fire, taken from the altar of Zeus at Mount Olympus in Athens and carried by torch runners, finally makes its way in a dramatic ceremony to light the flame that begins the games. Frankly folks, this is strange fire that would have brought on even more fireworks had it occurred in the camp of Israel in the Old Testament. God demanded that only fire that He himself started was to be used in the Tabernacle and anyone using any other fire would be killed. (Leviticus 10:1-2)

However, the torch run created so much excitement that other groups decided to do their own and more Christian version (whatever that is) of the run. One religious group used the torch to celebrate a milestone, a birthday of the group. The torch was to run from their organizational birthplace and eventually arrive at a conference in a city hundreds of miles away. The run, timed to culminate on a specific celebrative evening, arrived at the dramatic moment with the crowd in a high emotional state. One small problem: As the torch reached the stage and the crowd reached a crescendo, the fire went out.

Emotions fell as rapidly as they had risen. What were they to do now. It was a non-smoking group and no one had matches or a lighter, or at least no one would admit it. Finally, a convention center employee brought a match and the excitement, though not quite so intense and now carrying a humorous edge, returned.

Questions:

1. Can you think of other places or ways where we have Greek or Roman god names or practices?
2. What programs have collapsed at some point in your life? Was it embarrassing?

Embarrassment

Only two steps separated me from the front row of seats in this overcrowded college retreat in a beautiful area of the northern United States. It was heaven to me because I love speaking to collegians and love being that close to the people. This college retreat fulfilled my requirements for perfection and I gloated in the joy.

The front row, as usual, lined up the most intense and interested people. It also held one or two very *interesting* people. Seated those two steps away and slightly to my right was a person who had the perfect unisex look. One could not discern whether it was male or female. Full cut clothing and hair style masked all clues. Though I wondered, it presented no problem to me until one fateful moment I shall never forget.

Speakers frequently borrow phrases and actions from other speakers when they feel it will enhance the eloquence of the moment. Plagiarism was not beneath me at that time (or, frankly, now). In an effort to increase the drama of the moment, I borrowed a statement from a well-known (at least to that crowd) radio evangelist as I walked up to this unisex person and stated, "And that goes for you, too, Sir!"

Now, under ordinary circumstances and mental stability, this should present no problem; however, in the guilty realization that this phrase did not belong to me, my subproductive brain informed me that perhaps I had made a major goof and this person was not a sir. I am now convinced that this event would have faded from my memory and theirs had I merely advanced to my next point without further rumination, but it was too late.

To my own shock, I attempted to cover this bumbling slight to the person as I blurted out, "or Madam!" I knew from experience that I must grab control of my message and go on lest I be lost, but my mind sucked me down a bottomless pit. I knew that if the person were a female, she likely would not have been too offended by being called "Sir." Most girls live in peace with gender generics. However, I thought that if it was a male, the male ego was less likely to be receptive to being called "Madam." Instant sweat and instant insanity. I could not leave well enough alone.

I bumbled once again, blurting out, "Or whatever!" I instantly knew that no matter what he/she was, the term "whatever" would be unacceptable and totally offensive. I longed for some clue from the person's face with each term. Perhaps the eyes would light up when I spoke the appropriate word, although the humor of eyes lighting up at the word "whatever" almost made me lose further control.

Now, my mind swirled with the problem of my faux pas. I barely remained on any semblance of a track as I finished my message. I constantly searched the face of the person seated only two steps away for signs of displeasure. Deadpan! I longed for a shovel with which to dig my own hole and crawl in it. Misery.

Afterward, I struck up a conversation with the person, probing, grasping for a clue to gender. None was forthcoming. Any negative (or positive) reaction to my statement was carefully masked. I did not know what to do. Pain stalked me. I watched carefully from a distance to see what group this person would seek. No clues. Always a mixture. I could not ask anyone the gender, because that question would ultimately get back to the person, and my sin would be compounded.

Only the plane flight away provided relief. However, notice that now, 25 years later, the quest remains.

True relief still waits.

Questions:

1. Are you free to describe your most embarrassing moment? What was it?
2. Have you ever tried to correct something and ended up creating more problems for yourself? Describe.

Evil Empire

My first trip to Russia occurred shortly after the collapse of Communism. For a long time, we all knew that this Godless system had to fall. Ronald Reagan spoke truly when he called it "The Evil Empire." I was about to see for myself.

To get to the Black Sea where a Discipleship Training School of Youth With A Mission gathered, I flew to Moscow and connected on to Sotchi. As we landed in Moscow, row upon row of parked passenger jets lined the edge of the airport—silent testimony to a bankrupt system that could no longer afford fuel or parts.

The Moscow International Airport lacked convenient public transport into town, so friends met and took me to a place to spend the night. Then I discovered that the domestic airport lay completely across town and out in the country. I wondered, then found out why. I realized Communists did not want their people to travel, so they made it as difficult as possible. Further, they wanted to keep constant track of people and such separated airports made that task easier.

The next day, the long ride to the domestic terminal drove the realization further home. They especially didn't want foreign tourists (spies?) traveling in their country. I would soon find out how they handled them. I think they were embarrassed that we might see the truth of their poverty. The taxi ride had its own thrills. In the taxi, we ventured further and further from town, out into sheer country and then up a lonely forest-enclosed road, I began to wonder if either the driver did not understand where I wanted to go or if he was taking me out to rob and abandon me.

But sure enough, we turned into a large virtually empty parking lot with a large airport terminal. I watched the two main entrances for a while, finally deciding which one was for departure and entered. No crowd and no check-in counters. I stood in the center of the hall and studied the sparse flight schedule on the electronic board. Finally, I deciphered the Sotchi flight, but I saw no information to help me take the next step. I stood there for a long while and tried to think logically having been in enough airports in my life to give it a try. Nothing clicked.

I approached people walking in and asked if they spoke English. "Nyet, Nyet." Finally, a man who barely spoke any English pointed me outside and to the left. I walked out and saw a plain door obviously for employees or maintenance and walked back inside more confused than before. I walked to a door that others were going through thinking that maybe the gates were behind that door.

I opened the door and closed it quickly. That brief moment gave me a vision of the end of the world as I looked upon a mass of people and heard and saw what, in my scariest imagination, must approximate "weeping and wailing and gnashing of teeth." I stepped back, sweating and breathing harder. If I had to navigate that crowd, I needed some prayer and clarity of mind. I walked back to my "middle of the hall" position and stared at the door. The agony behind that door overwhelmed me. What was I going to do?

Once again, I sought English speakers. Once again, one of them pointed me outside and to the left. This time, I decided to forget the obvious and give it a try. I opened the plain, unidentified door and walked into a world of carpet, quiet, souvenirs and "Visa Card Welcome" signs. Then I remembered the old "Intourist" system whereby the Communists appointed a guide to each person visiting from the West, and that guide made sure that the visitor was exposed only to special rooms designed to impress and make him think that Communism was a lovely success. Such a huge, expensive lie!

I walked down the carpeted hall to a check-in counter. Only one person was ahead of me and in just minutes, I was checked in and held a boarding pass. The agent directed me upstairs to a restaurant and waiting area. I marveled at the contrast I had just observed. Heaven for the outsider; Hell for the insider. By now, my thirst drove me into the restaurant. I sat down in the available seat across from a well-dressed businessman. Soon we were in conversation. He worked for British Petroleum and was flying into the interior of the country.

The intercom interrupted our conversation. My flight to Sotchi would be delayed by twenty minutes. "Twenty minutes" seems to be the international airline opening salvo that usually ends up with "forever."

The businessman smiled at my concern and began his horror stories. "The last time I had a twenty-minute delay, I was here three days waiting. And you have to wait here in the lounge. You cannot leave."

"Why?" I asked.

"Usually," he continued, "the flight is delayed for lack of fuel, but it may go at any time, so you dare not leave."

My heart sank. I knew that any delay would destroy my whole trip and I had no way to inform those who would be meeting me. After just ten minutes, the Sotchi flight was announced and I cheerily headed to the security gate. Weary, bedraggled people passed by me as I walked. I spotted some American students with back packs. "So our Sotchi flight is almost on time. Great."

"Oh, no," they quickly answered. "This is the flight from two days ago and it is just now leaving." I gulped and walked back to the restaurant.

By now, I was looking for good sleeping places and thinking about food. This could be an adventure I had not foreseen. However, to my pleased surprise, my Sotchi flight was announced and I began my trek through security to the plane. I walked outside to a large plane-parking lot and found mine only because people were walking toward it. I kept repeating the word "Sotchi?" as I walked, looking for nodding heads of approval.

The plane held as many surprises for me as the terminal. This was Aeroflot! Perhaps that is all I need to say. All Westerners were seated together on the same row where all the seat belts and seat backs worked. I noticed others that did not work. The overhead compartment shocked me most. Rather than the compartment with a door as on all US airlines, it was merely an open bench. Large pieces of luggage hung out over the seats. One good air pocket and there would be fatalities. However, just as much luggage filled the aisles. This would be an adventure.

My mouth watered as I smelled some roasted chicken. I thought that maybe a meal would redeem this flight. Then I spotted the chicken on open paper in the lap of a passenger two rows behind me. He was the smart one. Service on the airplane consisted of three trips by the crew down the aisle. One was to sell newspapers. Another to sell lottery tickets. A third to give a glass of weak flavored water.

When we landed at Sotchi, we didn't actually land—we semi-crashed. We Westerners looked at each other as if "This is it!" Other passengers were unconcerned.

I walked with everyone to the luggage conveyer under an open roof area similar to a fairground cattle barn. Conveyer might be stretching it a little. More like a place where luggage could be shoved. My luggage did not arrive. Sweats again, until I realized that there must be a "nice" place where my luggage would be placed. Sure enough, I walked up the way to an attractive entrance and there, amid more conveniences, was my luggage and the person waiting to meet me. But I was glad that I had the opportunity to see how they treated the normal Russian passengers. By now, I had come to a firm conclusion: I was observing The Evil Empire!

The scenery became more pleasant as we journeyed by train to our port town where the school was being held. After all, this is an elite resort town on the Black Sea!

While at the port town, I made further discoveries. To make a phone call, one had to go to the post office, book a call and pay for it; and, at the appointed time, return to receive the call as placed by an official. All phone calls went through Moscow, even if to a neighboring town. That way, with one switch, the Communist leaders could disable the whole country's communication.

Also, I discovered that Russian women must shop constantly. Why? Consumer goods are scarce; food delivery irregular. When items became available they had to snap them up because they might not be available when they actually needed them. A Russian department store does not place items out where you can touch them. They are displayed behind glass or on walls behind counters. You point out what you want; and, if it is available, they will hand it to you. Now, with my own eyes, I had seen the fruit of The Evil Empire!

Questions:

1. If you are from the "Cold War" age, what promises do you remember that Communism made to people?
2. What do you think the world will be like when Jesus reigns?

Rain On Parades

I settled into my aisle seat to fly from Kona, Hawaii back to Los Angeles. A slightly disheveled wisp of a young lady slumped into the window seat and curled up into a fetal position. Pulling the thin airline blanket over herself, she looked at me and said, "I'm depressed and haven't had any sleep for two days. Please don't talk to me."

Since she opened/closed the conversation, I risked a question. "That is a tough combination. What brought it about?" She uncurled slightly and answered, "I am an astronomer. Everyone in the world wants to get on the Keck telescope. After years of application, I finally achieved a two-hour slot on the telescope and it was cloudy for the whole two hours. I am bummed."

After a short explanation of her planned observation, she drifted off into sleep. I pondered her scene and wondered how I would feel if my life's goal, my dream parade, was rained out. The joy of serving the Lord flows from the knowledge that even the rain fulfills his purposes. What I perceive as failure may be the greatest victory. Chance becomes purpose; coincidence becomes miracle.

I remembered this encounter of years ago because of a recent article in the Los Angeles Times. Another lady astronomer has discovered, using the Keck telescope, that stars are double stars as they are "formed" which, in evolutionary terms, means that planets are impossible. Which means our solar system is unique. Which means it must have been created. Hmmm. The whole evolutionary parade seems to be getting rained on.

Questions:

1. What great ambitions of yours have proven unattainable?
2. What unexpected rewards have you received from God that had you "singing in the rain"?

Rufus

Rufus Bohannon and Charlie Brown spent hours together. They were best friends. Charlie was my father-in-law. Both were godly men and leaders in the same church. Rufus, whom I knew well, had one interesting quirk. Whenever the sermon started, he went to sleep. It mattered not how interesting the speaker nor how loudly he held forth. Rufus would be sound asleep.

One particular Sunday, sleep came a bit early for Rufus. Much too early. As the pastor prepared to receive the morning's offering, he decided to ask Rufus to pray for the offering. Rufus was asleep. His wife, sitting right beside him, jabbed him in the ribs. Rufus awoke with a start and looked quizzically at his wife. She merely whispered, "Pray." Rufus rose to the task, immediately stood and dismissed everybody. The offering continued amidst the laughter.

Charlie and Rufus frequently got together for chat times. I hear them talking away in the living room, then silence. I check on them and find them both asleep. (Charlie was a sleepy-head too.) Then, after a short nap, they awaken and continue the conversation right where they left off.

Charlie and Rufus died within twenty-four hours of each other and were both in the same funeral home at the same time. I figured they said, "Let's take a little longer nap and continue up there where we don't have to stop."

Questions:

1. Do you have anyone you often just chat with? How did that relationship develop?
2. Have you ever had anything embarrassing happen to you in church? Tell about it.

Watch Your Head

Being only five feet, eight inches tall protects me from the normal worries of all you tall people. For instance, most beds are long enough for me and most "watch your head" signs can be ignored. My feet reach the floor, so I consider my legs long enough.

Once, in my life, I found my height to be a problem. I traveled to northern Thailand to speak at a pastors' conference held at a campground surrounding a soccer field. My room was a hut on the southern side of the field across from the open-air meeting hall. My bed—a mat on the floor under mosquito netting. The toilet—a small facility about 100 yards away.

God blessed me with a lot of energy that begins early in the day. I awakened each morning and bounded up from my mat, forgetting that the open rafters of the ceiling were made for Thailanders, not me. Wham! My ears rang and unusual sights swirled around my eyes. Too dazed to even cry out, I would go sit in the corner and wait for clarity to return and the pain to subside. It seemed that the blow would also knock the memory out of me and each day repeated the "wham, groan, sit" drama.

Add to this the fact that I had not been careful about my eating and drinking. Maybe it was the red ant eggs. I don't know. But by the third day, hourly visits provided great familiarity with the toilet, a hole in the ground over which you squat. One small problem—the door needed a "mind your head" sign, although I am not sure it would have helped me, especially in the middle of the night. Wham! Now, when your intense need for the toilet is intersected by pain and minimized consciousness, you invent a whole new set of problems to consider. Unusual prayers like "God, don't let me knock my brains out over here" flow from your lips.

When I returned home scratched and battered, it took answers to several suspicious questions before I could convince my wife that I had not been in a fight.

Questions:

1. Does your body size or shape ever present problems for you? When and how?
2. What foods have you heard of that you think you would refuse to eat?

Happy Trails

I joined the headquarters staff of a denomination to develop a new magazine for youth and some new youth programming. The new magazine I had in mind exceeded the skills of any designers I knew. Miraculously, God sent an outstanding designer named Dempster Evans. When I saw his work, I invited him to be the designer of the new magazine and he accepted. This was in 1969.

Dempster flew in every other month from California and we designed two issues of the magazine. He always brought news of the latest happenings in the Jesus Movement. The glowing reports fell on my skeptical ears. Many glowing reports of past revivals disappointed me upon closer examination or in the long run. But then, he began bringing newspaper clippings with photos of what was happening at Calvary Chapel of Costa Mesa. Being an old newspaper man, I knew these were not press releases but actual news. My interest increased.

"Why don't you come out and see for yourself? We can design issues out there as easy as here." That challenge by Dempster was all I needed. When I arrived, he told me we needed to get to church at least an hour early to get a seat, hopefully near the front. I was amazed. Before, if I went to church early it was to get rear seats. I was intrigued.

We managed to get seats near the middle on that Wednesday night. Bodies occupied every available space whether pew or floor—strange looking bodies. Clothing ran the range of styles. This was "hippie" territory. The stage was bare, containing only one stand mike. No thrones or decorations. The crowd chattered away excitedly. I liked what I was feeling.

A young man with a guitar walked out to the mike and, without saying anything, began a worship chorus. Instantly, the crowd quieted and joined in. Often, when we stood and sang, they would wrap their arms around each other and sway as one unit. At the close of each song, they all raised their hands in the "one way" sign.

The speaker that night looked like an explosion of hair and gunny sack cloth. His simple message said, "If you are living together and get saved, you need to get married." At the close, he stated that if anyone wanted to get saved to stand up. One hundred people stood! No push. No stories. No manipulation. In the applause and hugs that followed those who stood, I was willing to stand myself, so thrilling this event.

The next night, the scene repeated itself. This time, the pastor, Chuck Smith, dressed in a simple turtle-neck shirt, came out and sat on the floor of the platform during worship. That was new to me, but I liked it. At the close of his simple message, "The Bible Is the Word of God," another 100 people stood for salvation. By this point, I was overwhelmed watching something I had dreamed about all my life. I cried like a baby. Now I was putting it all together.

1. Everything was natural. Nothing fancy at all. Even the speech was natural. No preacher twang.
2. Worship was simply that! No cheerleading. No pressure. The leader worshipped and we joined him.
3. A well-thumbed Bible was in every hand and the sermons followed it closely.
4. The call for salvation was straightforward and without trickery, manipulation or any psychological gimmicks.
5. Everyone, regardless of looks or anything else, was welcomed.
6. Jesus was the center of everything and deeply loved.
7. The love that flowed to each other was overwhelming.

Well, in coming to California, I didn't leave my heart in San Francisco, I left it in Costa Mesa. Four years later, I moved there, and, if you receive my newsletter, you know that my relationship with Calvary Chapels (now a movement) has only grown. It has been a happy trail.

Questions:

1. What is the greatest church experience you have had?
2. Describe any events or discoveries that seemed to fulfill your dreams.

Those Floating Machines

As one pilot described flying as hours of boredom with moments of sheer terror, so many of us live routine lives with only moments of muscle vibrating terror. Sometimes we merely call them "close calls." At such times, if nothing else, we recognize our own vulnerability and mortality. Sometimes, also, these close calls come at times of high pleasure.

My brother, J.M., and I enjoyed sailing together whenever I visited him at his home on the Gulf of Mexico. Those moments were among my highest, especially one night as we sailed home on a warm sea. Plankton, glowing plankton, filled the water and illuminated our trail. We both broke into praise as two porpoises decided to join our sail. As brilliant glowing torpedoes they swam inches away on either side of us. Never seen such a sight before or after.

Our sailing brought about another event that became legendary in our household. Whenever we sailed, my mother would begin immediate intense prayer. She would call the Coast Guard and tell them, "Gentlemen, start your engines. The Erwin boys are on the ocean." The reason for this is that we would always run aground and have to be rescued. The reason for that is that my brother would turn the helm over to me. Though his instructions seemed simple, the top of the ocean looked the same everywhere to me. Also, there seemed to be more than one light to follow out there. Some were different colors, some blinked and some of them even moved. My incompetence bore its fruit.

One such episode almost ended all of our sailing. We sailed along the coast until we came into Lake Pontchartrain where we planned to dock the boat for the night. A breeze pushed us merrily along though we knew an approaching storm line was cause for some haste. We did not beat the storm. About a mile or two from the safe harbor, the wind began to blow us in first one way then the other. We could not get any speed in order to use our rudder before the wind would shift again. This troubled us. Then, absolute calm. That brought greater frustration with the harbor so close. We were pointed that direction but totally becalmed. Night enveloped us. J.M. stood at the bow. I sat at the stern with my hand on the rudder.

Suddenly, a powerful gust of wind hit our hanging sails with such a force that the front wire to the top of the mast snapped. The force splintered the tall wooden mast at its base and shot the sharp splinters straight toward my brother while the top came crashing down toward me. With only millimeters to spare, it missed us, but we both could have been killed at that one moment.

Now, drifting powerlessly, the wind driving us toward shore where the boat would be beaten to splinters by the waves, we hastily brought up a small outboard motor to attach to the back and hope that it was stronger than the wind. The first job was to get the wires and sails out of the water so they would not entangle the propeller. With that finally done and the shore coming rapidly upon us, we cranked furiously on the motor but it refused to start.

My brother headed into the hold of the boat with a hatchet to beat a hole in the hull to sink the boat. It would be easier to raise and repair it later than to salvage its remains from the shore. Just before he began to hack away, one more crank produced the relieving whine of the motor. Though it was barely stronger than the wind, we inched our way into a safe-harbor marina amid frequent expressions of thanks to God for what we considered to be a series of miracles.

⌒

Dempster Evans (the designer of Youth Alive Magazine and the man who introduced me to Calvary Chapel) was going to be in New Orleans and I in Mississippi, so we decided to get together on the Coast and design two issues of the magazine.

We developed a glorious plan. We would have my brother, J.M., take us out on his sailboat into the Gulf of Mexico near a barrier island, anchor us there with provisions and motor back in on a small skiff. Days later he would return to bring us back.

There, in the pleasantness of gulf breezes and away from all distractions, our creative juices flowed freely. On our first day, after a design session that produced so much we dared not stop, we were mentally coasting at midnight on the deck before retiring. Moonlight made the sea magical. We decided that all magazine design should occur this way.

Shortly before we began our relaxation time, a strange wind blew in that couldn't seem to decide what direction it wanted to go. I remembered that the boat seemed to go in circles around the anchor spot. Now, though the breeze had settled to one direction, it still blew with briskness. As we sat in the strength of the moonlight, I noticed a buoy, a channel marker that I didn't remember in our sight when we anchored. I remarked to Dempster that it was most unusual to see a channel marker broken loose from its mooring and floating. As it floated by us, automatic thinking took over. I realized that if it was loose, it was floating against the wind and current. Then I knew. We were loose and floating by the marker!

This required immediate emergency action. We were in danger of hitting the island and being destroyed on the shore. I had only minutes to respond. First, I must start the engine. My brother had carefully shown me how to do that before he motored away. Then we had to raise the anchor and get the boat turned back toward the channel. Forging against the current, the engine strained every muscle as we pulled the anchor in. The circling boat had wrapped the line around the anchor yielding it useless.

Now, powered and underway, where do we go? Roads in the ocean don't have centerline stripes. I knew that to move back straight toward the city would run us aground. I headed toward the nearest flashing light. Then on to the next flashing light. When we arrived at the final light, I could see the lights of Pascagoula, Mississippi and I knew we were in the right channel.

I eased slowly into the harbor and with mild panic inched up to the dock of the harbor police. When we safely tied up and stopped the engine, I don't remember ever heaving such a sigh of relief. From a pay phone inside I called my brother, J.M. A glance at my watch showed it to be 3:00 a.m.

"J.M."

"Hello, Gayle. GAYLE!!! Where are you? What are you doing? How did you call me?"

He picked us up and we spent the remainder of the night washing salt water out of our minds. However, though with only one evening afloat, the designs and ideas we developed were used profitably for years.

Questions:

1. Describe some times you felt you were in great danger and God rescued you.
2. What are your favorite times of recreation? Does your recreation ever create any side problems such as soreness, expense, etc.? What are they?

Tsk, Tsk, Gayle

High School provided the best teacher I ever had. World class in his effectiveness, he was the reason I majored in chemistry in college.

However, one particular practice of his fell far beneath my "favorite" line. Every six weeks, when he assigned new grades, he seated us in the class/laboratory in accordance with our grade. Top grade occupied right front seat. Students were then seated in descending order all the way to idiot's row.

One time(!) I made it. Top grade! I will never forget the day. He placed me in the first seat. I waited patiently while he seated the "lesser ones." When he finished and turned to come to the front to continue his lecture, the door opened and in walked a transfer student from another city. He looked at her and said, "Oh my, this class moves like lightning. You are months behind already. You need to sit right up front where you can see everything.... Gayle?"

I got up, gave her my seat and walked back to the only seat available in idiot's row. It would have been OK, except that everyone in the school knew how he seated people and when anyone came into the room, they would look around and say to me, "Tsk, Tsk, Gayle."

I did everything to prove that I didn't belong back there. Every question asked, I tried to answer. I was obnoxious. I understand the Apostle

Peter much better now in his impetuousness as he attempted to gain the upper hand in the fight to determine the greatest in the kingdom.

Questions:

1. What types of things do you do to improve your noticeability?
2. What, if any, honors would you be willing to decline?

The Story Story

Behind all these stories rests one overriding fact that fuels all of it—I am a follower of Jesus. My walk with Him has opened more doors than I could ever walk through, put me around more people than I could ever meet and brought me far more acquaintances than I could ever call confidants. Walking with Jesus has meant more fulfillment than any one person ever deserves and more adventure than one mind can dream up.

This Christ-walk created empathy and compassion otherwise impossible for me and altered all my ambitions. At his call, the ambitions of my youth were abandoned joyfully for a far greater goal. Not one subsequent experience ever awakened a remorse or longing for the past. In spite of all the difficulties, even tragedies, that I have known as a person and family member, not one event has touched the joy that resides in my heart. I am a happy man. I wish all people were as happy as I.

In fact, if there were one heresy I would like to believe, it is that all people would be saved. However, God honors the choices of people and will force no one into his heaven.

Nonetheless, the one overriding goal of my life is that all who hear my voice might know Him. That includes you, as the reader of this page. If you will listen to the hunger of your heart, the wisdom of the ages and the gentle pull of the One who loves you most, please begin your greatest story now by simply confessing your belief in Jesus as the Son of God and redeemer of your soul.

Welcome to the Family. The party starts now. The story will never end.

–Gayle D. Erwin

If you choose to follow Jesus after reading this, please write to me at Box 219, Cathedral City, CA 92235. I would like to send you some encouraging material.

Other Books and Resources by Gayle Erwin

The Jesus Style
A unique look at the real Jesus. In 20 languages and 40 printings, this hallmark book remains the book of choice for reading and giving to others.

The Father Style
This book breaks new ground in seeing God the Father through the eyes of Jesus. You will know Him and love Him.

The Spirit Style
The Holy Spirit through the prophecies and life of Jesus. A healing and resolving book.

That Reminds Me of a Story
Forty true and unique stories from the life and observation of Gayle Erwin. This book taps the whole range of emotions.

Video and Audio Tapes
A rich and extensive group of teachings by Gayle. His delightful insight and humorous approach to Scripture make these very popular to all ages.

Servant Quarters
This magazine/newsletter contains his latest writings, news and reader response. Sent free or read on our website.

To order or receive a catalog, write:
Servant Quarters, Box 219, Cathedral City, CA 92235
or call toll free 1-888-321-0077

Website: www.servant.org

Email: gayle@servant.org

Gayle Erwin has spent 43 years as a pastor, college teacher, evangelist and magazine creator and editor. He devotes his time now to teaching and writing about the nature of Jesus.

Bonus Story

The plane had landed and emptied in Rochester, New York, on my flight from Toronto to Philadelphia. A clean-cut couple boarded the plane carrying a chubby infant and leading a three- or four-year-old little girl. About three rows behind me, they seated the daughter next to the window and fastened their seat belts.

Other passengers, bedraggled and weary from a day's work, began dragging themselves and their luggage down the aisle. Suddenly, over the clatter of baggage being stowed, I heard the delightful sound of a little girl singing to the top of her voice, "Jesus loves me, this I know, for the Bible tells me so!"

My heart and my face broke into a smile. It was the finest moment I have had on USAir.